MASTER THE

AP* GOVERNMENT & POLITICS TESTS

Joan U. Levy, Ph.D.
Norman Levy, Ph.D.
Rafael Katz, M.A.

TEACHER-TESTED STRATEGIES AND TECHNIQUES FOR SCORING HIGH

2002

ARCO
THOMSON LEARNING™

Australia • Canada • Mexico • Singapore • Spain • United Kingdom • United States

An ARCO Book

ARCO is a registered trademark of Thomson Learning, Inc., and is used herein under license by Peterson's.

About Peterson's

Founded in 1966, Peterson's, a division of Thomson Learning, is the nation's largest and most respected provider of lifelong learning resources, both in print and online. The Education Supersite℠ at www.petersons.com—the Internet's most heavily traveled education resource—has searchable databases and interactive tools for contacting U.S.-accredited institutions and programs. In addition, Peterson's delivers unmatched financial aid resources and test-preparation tools. Peterson's serves more than 100 million education consumers annually.

Peterson's is a division of Thomson Learning, one of the world's largest providers of lifelong learning. Thomson Learning serves the needs of individuals, learning institutions, and corporations with products and services for both traditional and distributed learning. Headquartered in Stamford, Connecticut, with offices worldwide, Thomson Learning is a division of The Thomson Corporation (www.thomson.com), one of the world's leading e-information and solutions companies in the business, professional, and education marketplaces. For more information, visit www.thomsonlearning.com.

For more information, contact Peterson's, 2000 Lenox Drive, Lawrenceville, NJ 08648;
800-338-3282; or find us on the World Wide Web at: www.petersons.com/about

ISBN: 0-7689-0736-5

Printed in the United States of America

10 9 8 7 6 5 4 3 2 1 03 02 01

Table of Contents

About the Authors

JOAN U. LEVY, Ph.D.

Director of NJL College Preparation. Guidance Counselor and Educational Evaluator for the New York City Board of Education with 19 years of teaching and guidance experience. Former Adjunct Instructor of Education at the Master's degree level. B.A., City College of New York; M.S. in Guidance and Counseling, Fordham University; Ph.D. in Behavioral Science.

NORMAN LEVY, Ph.D.

Executive Director of NJL College Preparation, a private tutoring, test preparation, and college guidance service. Teaching experience in the public and private sectors. B.E., City College of New York; M.S. in Operations Research, New York University; Ph.D. in Educational Administration.

RAFAEL KATZ, M.A.

B.A. in History and Chinese, Brown University; M.A. in Asian Studies, Yale University. Teacher at high school and college levels in the U.S. and in Taiwan.

Introduction

What Is the Advanced Placement (AP)* Program?

The Advanced Placement (AP) Program is a way for high school students to study college-level material and receive college credit for their efforts. It is administered by the College Board, which contracts with the Educational Testing Service (ETS) for the Advanced Placement examinations. The Advanced Placement Program is a way for stronger students to study courses appropriate to their abilities and interests and be fairly certain that they will not have to repeat these courses on the college level. Students are selected for Advanced Placement courses on the basis of a number of criteria determined by their high school. These criteria may include the following:

- Scholastic record
- Interview and acceptance by the teacher
- Score on nationally normed examinations like PSAT/NMSQT
- Parental approval
- Volunteer record

In any school year, you may take as many AP exams as you want with certain limitations. You may take one of each of the following, but no two exams in one subject:

- Computer Science A *or* Computer Science AB
- Calculus AB *or* Calculus BC
- Physics B *or* Physics C
- Studio Art (Drawing Portfolio *or* General Portfolio)

* Advanced Placement Program is a registered trademark of the College Entrance Examination Board, which does not endorse this book.

In Which Courses Are Advanced Placement Credits Offered?

The AP Program now exists for the following courses:

ART	History	
	Studio Art	Drawing Portfolio 2-D Portfolio; 3-D Portfolio
BIOLOGY	Biology	
CALCULUS	AB;BC	
CHEMISTRY	Chemistry	
COMPUTER SCIENCE	A AB	
ECONOMICS	Microeconomics Macroeconomics	
ENGLISH	Language and Composition Literature and Composition	
ENVIRONMENTAL SCIENCE	Environmental Science	
FRENCH	Language Literature	
GERMAN	Language	
GEOGRAPHY	Human Geography	
GOVERNMENT and POLITICS	Comparative United States	
HISTORY	European United States World	
LATIN	Literature Virgil	
MUSIC	Theory	
PHYSICS	B	
	C	Electricity and Magnetism Mechanics
PSYCHOLOGY	Psychology	
SPANISH	Literature Language	
STATISTICS	Statistics	

What is an AP Examination Like?

Each year in early May, AP examinations are given. Most students can take the exams in their own schools.

Each AP examination is a comprehensive evaluation of the subject matter. It may consist of objective questions, essays, data-based questions, and portfolio evaluations. Objective questions require you to choose the correct response from several choices. Free-response questions (including essay and data-based questions) require you to arrange your knowledge and write clear, well-organized answers.

How Are AP Examinations Scored and Reported?

AP examinations are scored on a five-point scale:

Grade	Verbal Equivalent
5	Extremely well-qualified
4	Well-qualified
3	Qualified
2	Possibly qualified
1	No recommendation

Colleges that accept Advanced Placement courses usually accept grades of 3 or better. In order to earn a part score that is equivalent to a total grade of 3, you must answer approximately 50 to 60 percent of the multiple-choice questions correctly.

AP grade reports, together with candidate rosters and interpretive information, are sent in early July to the colleges chosen by the candidates. Transcripts can later be sent to other colleges for a $12.00 fee. Grade reports are sent only to colleges the candidate has designated. Grades are also sent to the students and to their high schools. In August, schools receive their AP Teacher Reports comparing their pupils' performance to that of the total candidate group on each examination.

What AP Dates Should I Be Aware of?

February	Deadline for finding the local schools that administer AP examinations
March	Schools hand in Examination and Special Services Order Forms and Fee Reduction Request Forms
April	Intensive review for Examinations
Early May Mid-May	Examination weeks
June	June 15—Deadline for receipt of letters asking for changes in reporting grades to college
July	AP Grade Reports are given to selected colleges, to the student, and to the high school

What Are the Benefits of the Advanced Placement Program?

The AP Program offers a number of benefits to its participant students:

1. It allows high school students to master more challenging course work in areas of interest and proficiency. It also gives students time to explore college subject areas while still in high school.
2. It permits students to take college-level courses and, if they do well on the AP examination and attend a participating university or college, receive course credit for their work.
3. It provides tuition savings for students. They may receive up to a year of credit for three or more qualifying AP grades.
4. Studies have shown that qualified candidates go on to complete undergraduate programs of real strength, generally achieving records superior to those obtained by students whose basic college courses were taken at the college level.
5. It opens eligibility for honors and other special programs to students who have received AP recognition.

What Are the Fees for AP Examinations?

The current fee for each examination is $77.00. In one year you may take as many AP examinations as you choose with certain limitations. You may take only one examination from each of the following four subject areas:

- Computer Science (A *or* AB)
- Mathematics (Calculus AB *or* Calculus BC)
- Physics (B *or* C)
- Studio Art (General *or* Drawing)

You may take either or both examinations from the following four subject areas for one fee:

- Physics C (Mechanics *and/or* Electricity and Magnetism)
- Latin (Virgil *and/or* Catullus–Horace)
- Government and Politics (Comparative *and/or* United States)
- Economics (Microeconomics *and/or* Macroeconomics)

You may take either or both examinations from the following five subject areas, but you must pay a separate fee for each:

- Spanish (Language *and/or* Literature)
- French (Language *and/or* Literature)
- History (European *and/or* United States)
- English (Language and Composition *and/or* Literature and Composition)
- Art (History *and/or* Studio Art)

Fees are submitted to the AP Coordinator of the school giving the examination, according to the instructions that accompany the Order Forms.

For students with financial need, a reduced fee of $44.00 per test is available.

Once an examination is begun, you are ineligible for a refund of the $77.00 fee. However, if the examination is not begun, you may request a refund from the AP Coordinator.

Are Special Arrangements Available to Students with Disabilities?

If testing modifications are necessary, you should notify the AP Coordinator before December 1 of the school year in which you are taking the exam. There are two different accommodates that are available—those that can be made with standard timed conditions and those that will require the exam to be marked as "nonstandard administration."

For additional information, contact the College Board at ssd@info.collegeboard.org, or by mail at College Board Services for Students with Disabilities, P.O. Box 6226, Princeton, NJ 08541-6226.

How Can the Grades Be Used?

There are a number of different approaches to the AP score, depending on the college that you plan to attend:

- No credit is given.
- No credit is given; instead, advanced standing is given and you must take a more advanced course in that department.
- Credit is given in the major field of the examination, such as history.
- Credit is given for the course; you must now take a more advanced course in that department.
- Credit is given; you must pay for the credit hours obtained.
- Credit is given for only one introductory course in the major.
- Credit is given; the credits count towards the total needed for graduation.
- Credit is given for three or four AP scores; you now have sophomore standing, skipping freshman year and starting college as a sophomore.

Another way that the AP score can be used revolves around the CLEP examination. If your AP score was too low to allow college credit, you may take a College-Level Examination Program (CLEP) in American Government and may obtain college credit for the CLEP exam instead.

WHAT TO EXPECT

What Is the Format of the AP U.S. Government and Politics Exam?

The AP U.S. Government and Politics examination is a two-hour and twenty-five minute examination broken down as follows:

Type of Question	Time Allotted (minutes)	U.S. Government and Politics	
		Number of Questions	% of Grade
Multiple Choice	45	60	50
Free-response	45	4	50

MULTIPLE-CHOICE SECTION

The multiple-choice section of the AP U.S. Government and Politics examination consists of 60 questions testing the student's knowledge of basic concepts used to interpret and evaluate U.S. politics, and the assessment of specific case studies. The main content areas on the exam include:

Constitutional basis of U.S. government	5%–15% of the test
Political beliefs and actions of individuals	10%–20% of the test
Political parties, interest groups, and the media	10%–20% of the test
Congress, the presidency, the bureaucracy, and the courts	35%–45% of the test
Civil rights and civil liberties	5%–15% of the test

FREE-RESPONSE SECTION

The free-response section consists of four questions with 100 minutes allotted to complete them. Knowledge from different areas must be synthesized and applied to the questions. Students are required to exhibit their logical and organizational skills in explaining and/or evaluating principles of government and politics.

Students may be presented with a quotation, a chart, a graph, or other such political stimuli and asked to evaluate and analyze the data in light of their knowledge of U.S. government.

How is the Examination Graded?

Grading of the exam is as follows:

Multiple-choice questions —50% of the grade

Free-response and stimulus-based essay questions —50% of the grade

The AP U.S. Government and Politics examination is scored on a five-point scale as follows:

5—Extremely well-qualified

4—Well-qualified

3—Qualified

2—Possibly qualified

1—No recommendation

Should I Guess on AP Examination Multiple-Choice Questions?

The multiple-choice sections of AP examinations are based on the number of questions answered correctly minus a fraction of the number answered incorrectly. Thus with questions that have five answer choices, one-quarter of a point is subtracted for each incorrect answer. For questions with four answer choices, one-third of a point is subtracted for each incorrect answer. If you can eliminate one or more of the answer choices, it is desirable to guess. If not, it is better to skip the question.

How Do I Prepare Myself for the Test?

STUDY THE TEXTBOOK!

Notice that we said *study*, not *read*. The two terms are NOT interchangeable. Although it is hoped that the material that you read will enthrall you, it is foolish to conclude that the text will require no more effort than reading an interesting story or watching a good movie. Government and political science do not have nice neat plot lines like novels. The interrelationships among branches of government interact in complicated ways. Do not treat the text as a "light read."

Try to focus on the key events or ideas that are emphasized in the chapter assigned, which often appear in the title of the chapter, so they are not difficult to find.

Once the key point or points of the chapter are determined, the next step is to put that centerpiece in its proper setting. Train yourself to think about this particular issue in the context of the U.S. political system. Without seeing an event in context, the fact, no matter how important it may be, is meaningless.

PAY ATTENTION TO THE LECTURES!

This means not only taking notes in class but also studying those notes. An effective way to study is to transfer notes taken in class to a notebook kept at home. Rather than merely copying the notes, however, read them, digest the information, and then write a *condensed* version in your notebook. This takes a little longer, but the time needed for cramming later will be reduced.

WRITING THE ESSAYS

Writing essays is a key part of the AP exams, and of every AP course, a fact which is consistent with the idea that knowledge of events or thoughts in isolation is next to useless. As noted above, you should think about each event or thought in its "proper setting." You must see the issue in the context of our three branches of government. Each branch—legislative, executive, and judicial—has an impact on both the issue and on the other branches. It is extremely difficult to write a solid essay on any issue of importance without seeing the "larger picture."

In order to write a coherent essay, it is important not only to have a clear understanding of events and their meanings, but also to be able to present this understanding in an organized manner. Make an outline! In most cases, a chronological sequence makes sense. Finally, remember the advice that the king gave to Alice at the trial of the tarts: Start at the beginning, go through the middle, come to the end, and then stop!

PART 1

The Essay and the Free-Response Question

PREVIEW

Chapter 1

The Essay

Nothing strikes fear in the hearts of most high school students as much as writing an essay, especially one that constitutes a good part of the grade on an important exam. However, essay writing does not have to be frightening or terribly difficult.

The key to writing a good essay is *organization*. The essay on the AP U.S. Government and Politics examination is meant to be a persuasive essay. The writer espouses a point of view and gives evidence to support that point of view. Below are certain techniques that are helpful in writing the essay.

ROAD MAP

- *Steps in Writing a Persuasive Essay*
- *Scoring the Essay*

Steps in Writing a Persuasive Essay

1. SET UP AN OUTLINE CHART

Before you write a formal outline, a good brainstorming method is to set up an outline chart. Such a chart focuses you on all the information you will need to answer all the parts of a particular question. If a question asks you to discuss two examples, you will chart each example. Key words in a question, such as *discuss*, *show*, *tell*, *explain*, and *describe*, will guide you as to what to include in your outline chart.

Here is a sample chart:

Question: Discuss the influence of two Enlightenment philosophers on the creation of the Federal Constitution. Give several concrete examples for each philosopher's influence.

Enlightenment Philosopher	Examples of Constitutional Influence
	1. 2. 3.
	1. 2. 3.

2. PREPARE AN OUTLINE

Some students believe that an outline wastes valuable test time on an AP exam. On the contrary, an outline can actually save you time by organizing your thoughts before you begin to write your essay.

The outline functions as a rough guide to your presentation of material. It helps you include relevant material in appropriate places and provide a cogent, well-presented argument. The outline should be organized loosely as follows:

I. Introduction

A. Introduce the topic.

B. Provide some background information, if appropriate.

C. State the thesis (your point of view in the argument). The thesis is *essential* in a good persuasive essay.

II. Body

A. Provide specific examples to support the thesis.

B. Use documentary evidence, if applicable.

C. Utilize positive, as well as negative verification for the argument. Show not only why this thesis is plausible, but why other interpretations are not.

III. Conclusion

A. Summarize the information.

B. Restate the thesis.

The preceding outline can help in planning the paragraphs, in putting the evidence in the logical or chronological order, and in mapping out the strategy that will be most convincing.

3. WRITE THE ESSAY

Once the outline is written, the actual essay writing should be fairly straightforward. You should have the information and should know where you want to put each piece of support evidence. The thesis should be clear, and the examples, documentation, and/or arguments should follow in logical order.

Each discrete example belongs in its own paragraph; transitional words—*in addition, another, however, furthermore, moreover, therefore, thus, consequently, hence, etc.*—can be used to make one paragraph flow into the next one.

4. PROOFREAD THE ESSAY

This is a *crucial* step in writing a good essay. Make sure to take the time to read the essay over carefully. Use the following checklist:

—*Is everything spelled correctly?* Nothing looks worse on an essay than misspelled words. If you don't know how a word is spelled, use another in its place!

—*Are the sentences varied in sentence structure?* Try to use simple sentences, compound sentences, complex sentences, questions, and declarative statements. Make the essay interesting to the reader.

—*Is the essay grammatically correct?* Check subject-verb agreement, tense, plurals, etc.

—*Are the essay's arguments well presented?* Are they convincing? Do they support the thesis and argue their case well? Are any essential parts of the argument omitted?

Proofreading need not take a long time but can make a difference between a good essay and a superb one. Don't forget this essential step!

Scoring the Essay

This essay is scored on a 15-point scale as follows:

SCORES

1–3	Demonstrates incompetence	The student does not comprehend the question and addresses the issues in an inapplicable way.
4–6	Suggests incompetence	The student shows inadequate understanding of the question. Response is minimal.
7–9	Suggests competence	The student understands the question but does not develop it sufficiently.
10–12	Demonstrates competence	The student demonstrates an understanding of the question but presents an uneven argument for his or her point of view.
13–15	Demonstrates superiority	The student fully comprehends the question and delivers apt examples to defend his or her point of view.

The score for the essay is combined with the scores for the multiple-choice section and the stimulus-based free-response questions to produce one score for the exam as a whole.

Chapter

Ten Practice Essays

This chapter contains 10 practice essays similar to those found on the Advanced Placement (AP) U.S. Government and Politics examination. We suggest that you use the topics presented here to write your own essays before reading the samples. Remember to outline, write, and proofread! Then read the practice essays and compare yours to the ones given.

Question One

Various minority groups have worked toward improving their civil rights in the United States. They have employed a variety of methods to achieve their civil rights goals. In your essay, select TWO of the groups listed below and discuss the methods they have employed to influence government and to what degree they have been successful.

(A) African Americans
(B) women
(C) Hispanics
(D) elderly people
(E) people with disabilities

ANALYSIS OF QUESTION ONE

To answer this question well, the general concept of civil rights must be defined. Many students taking the exam would probably consider African Americans and women as being the easiest groups to write about, and it is true that textbooks and political writing in general have a plethora of information on these two subjects. If you are familiar with any of the other three choices, writing on one of them would suggest a more in-depth knowledge of civil rights issues. For any group that you choose, you should be sure that you have specific examples of how its members have worked to influence politics.

Another essential element of this question is familiarity with techniques used by interest groups to influence government. Good examples of these techniques might include the NAACP and their role in the Brown v. Board of Education of Topeka decision, the push by women's groups to pass the Equal Rights Amendment, or the lobbying that led to legislation requiring businesses with a certain number of workers to make the workplace accessible to those with disabilities.

FIRST ESSAY FOR QUESTION ONE

Women and African Americans are both groups that have struggled for civil rights. Taking into consideration slavery, segregation, and other forms of discrimination that have been institutionalized by the federal government, it would seem that African Americans' struggle for civil rights have been much more extensive than women's. On the other hand, if you take into consideration the fact that women's suffrage came a good 50 years after the Fourteenth and Fifteenth Amendments, which helped African Americans win the right to vote, it could be argued that some aspects of women's civil rights have been more neglected than the rights of African Americans.

Beginning with the Three-Fifths Compromise, which counted slaves as three-fifths of a person when calculating the number of representatives from different states, the institutions of American government have violated the civil rights of African Americans. Although the amendments that followed the Civil War corrected unfair aspects of the Constitution, the extent to which African Americans were actually treated as equal to whites varied from state to state and town to town. Jim Crow laws, grandfather clauses, and gerrymandering that purposely discouraged African-American districts are all examples of practices on state and local levels that maintained abuses in civil rights. It was not until the fifties and sixties that African Americans, under the leadership of such civil rights crusaders as Dr. Martin Luther King, Jr. and Malcolm X, launched protests and demonstrations that effectively turned the country's attention to their plight. A series of Supreme Court cases, most notably *Brown v. Board of Education of Topeka*, further helped the cause of African-American civil rights.

The women's civil rights movement was slow to get started partly because many men and women did not see that the civil rights of women were being violated. The suffrage movement of the early nineteenth century was one of the first organized grassroots efforts in which women demanded their rights. Even then, there were a number of women that did not agree with the suffragettes. The two world wars, especially the Second World War, gave women a new independence when they had to help the war effort by stepping in and doing traditionally male jobs. This newfound independence created a momentum for civil rights that has not stopped.

In the cases of both women and African Americans, the government in the form of new laws and protections and Supreme Court decisions adapted to reflect the demands made by both groups for civil rights. That is the job of democracy. After all, a basic function of a democracy is to defend the rights of minorities against tyranny by the majority.

CRITICAL COMMENTARY

This essay would receive the grade of 7. Although it lays out an argument and supports it, it tends to be a bit too historical and, more importantly, does not spend enough time on methods, which the question specifically asks for.

SECOND ESSAY FOR QUESTION ONE

Women have employed various methods to improve their civil rights in the last 150 years. The basic method used was the power of organizing. From Seneca Falls in 1848 to the present National Organization for Women, the feminist movement has gained strength through the power of mass organization.

However, only as women gained economic power have such organizations grown in influence. Women began entering the workforce in massive numbers after World War II. Today, women make up more than 50 percent of the total labor force in the United States. Therefore, they are now represented in many major occupational fields. Nevertheless, women are still underrepresented in the highest echelons of the corporate ladder and in government.

To change this, women have started using their economic and political power. They have organized to boycott the products of corporations that do not promote women to high executive positions and have used the courts to enforce affirmative action rules. Through various divisions of human rights, women have successfully sued when companies have had an established history of discrimination—especially in hiring and promotions. Where women have been less successful has been in the proving of sexual harassment because of definitional problems.

By far the most successful method women have used to further feminist causes has been the ballot. Polls have consistently shown than a gender gap exists. Women tend to vote for those candidates favoring such women's causes as abortion rights and increased spending for social programs such as day care and education. Women have established political action committees to elect such candidates and give support to a fresh crop of female candidates. This was shown in the last election, in which women made significant inroads in the House of Representatives and Senate as well as in their election to local government positions.

African Americans have also used a variety of ways to end political and economic segregation. After Reconstruction, the South established many laws to separate the races in terms of education and political accommodations. African-Americans were also forbidden by law and tradition from holding certain jobs.

One method African Americans used was the courts. Lawyers for the NAACP, such as Thurgood Marshall in the 1940s and 1950s, forced the courts to enforce civil rights laws passed during Reconstruction. This culminated in the landmark decision of *Brown v. Board of Education of Topeka*, declaring "separate but equal" education unconstitutional. However, progress was slow in desegregating southern schools. Since 1954, it has been easier to prove de jure segregation than de facto segregation—especially when many white parents have withdrawn their children from urban school systems.

To end segregation in public accommodations, African-Americans have used a variety of methods. By far the most successful was civil disobedience, as advocated by Dr. Martin Luther King, Jr. He organized sit-ins and boycotts of stores and transportation facilities. Demonstrations and picketing were also organized.

Political discrimination was ended only when a coalition of African-American religious groups, the NAACP, and white liberals lobbied Congress to pass various civil rights and voting rights legislation in the mid-1960s. These acts legally ended discrimination in public accommodations and allowed African-Americans to register in vast numbers, changing the political landscape of many urban areas north and south.

Though laws have been passed forbidding discrimination in housing and employment, many of these laws have been circumvented. Gentlemen's agreements and redlining have prevented African-Americans from moving into certain neighborhoods.

Affirmative action has been a mixed bag for African Americans. Though the EEOC has been successful in ending employment discrimination where there has been a long and proven history of it, there has been less success in trying to equalize employment in various industries. Many Americans are against quotas, and this has caused a backlash against many affirmative action programs.

Like women, African Americans have also tried to use the ballot to try to gain greater representation in Congress. However, they have been less successful than their female counterparts. African Americans have mostly been elected in those districts where the majority of the population are minorities. Nevertheless, African Americans in Congress have formed a black caucus to try to influence future legislation in which they are involved.

CRITICAL COMMENTARY

This is a comprehensive and very thorough essay. It discusses women and African Americans and the methods in which they influenced government. It also evaluates the relative success of each group.

Score: Demonstrates superiority

Question Two

Discuss the system of checks and balances and its effect on TWO of the following important tasks of government.

(A) creating and implementing the national budget
(B) improving education
(C) using the military to defend U.S. interests abroad
(D) building and repairing the transportation infrastructure

ANALYSIS OF QUESTION TWO

In the introduction to this essay, the writer first needs to define checks and balances. This is most effectively done with specific language and/or items from the Constitution that establish the checks and balances between the three branches of the U.S. government. Like all essays, choose the topics about which you know the most specific details. For any of the four topics you have to choose from, there are examples of the political battle between the president and Congress, and of times when the Supreme Court stepped in to settle disputes. Former President Bush's repeated request for a line-item veto and the Congress's refusal to grant it is an example of the Congress checking the president's power in the battle to control the budget. The War Powers Act is an example of the Congress trying to check the president's power as commander in chief.

FIRST ESSAY FOR QUESTION TWO

The framers of the Constitution created a system of checks and balances. It was built into the Constitution to guarantee that no one part of the government could become powerful enough to dominate the other parts. It is fair to say that a young nation, which still had the tyranny of George III of England in their memories when its representatives were creating the Constitution, structured the whole theory of government around checks and balances. As envisioned by Enlightenment luminary Montesquieu, checks and balances is a system where power checks power. It assumes that if executive and legislative powers are united in the same person, there can be no liberty. This is the basis of the Constitution.

When in actual use, the mechanics of checks and balances may often appear as a struggle in the upper echelons of government. It is not intended to create a harmonious system, so what observers might view as a struggling government is really a government with a premium on liberty working as it was designed. The expanding and contracting powers of the president to use America's military forces since World War II gives a good example of checks and balances in action. The Constitution created a situation where the Congress can check the president's power to wage war in two ways. First, the Senate must approve any declaration of war. Secondly, with the "power of the purse," Congress as a whole can decide what military items it will or will not fund.

Shortly after World War II, when the United States was in the midst of the Cold War, President Eisenhower requested a joint resolution from Congress to use military force to protect Taiwan, and he got it. In the same manner, the Gulf of Tonkin Resolution gave Presidents Nixon and Johnson unilateral war-making authority in Asia. With the War Powers Resolution came a check on the president's power, which balanced the ever-increasing power the president was accruing to wage war during the Cold War. The Congress, which in this case seemed to be more in concert with the country's weariness of the Vietnam War, passed the resolution, which prohibited the president from introducing troops into combat for more than 60 days without the Congress's approval. President Nixon used his check on the Congress's power to make legislation by using the veto. The Congress then took advantage of its own powers to control the presidency by overriding the president's veto. If one were to view these proceedings in a negative light, one could say that the Congress and the president were engaged in "in-fighting" over vital security issues, but as I have already argued, there is nothing in these proceedings that was not in line with Montesquieu's original plan for prevention of tyranny through checks and balances.

The annual struggle between the president and Congress over the budget is the system of checks and balances played out to its utmost. The ultimate power to pass a budget was invested in the Congress by the Constitution. As the budget deficit has grown in the 1980s and early 1990s, and Republican executives have differed with a Democrat-dominated legislature, the struggle of branch against branch has not always led to optimal results. But despite signs of the system not doing its job—pork-barrel spending and an ever-increasing deficit—it has for the most part lived up to the principles of checks and balances. More often than not, opposing branches of government have had to compromise so that a budget could be passed. What many look at as a serious breach of George Bush's campaign promise not to raise taxes in 1988, if looked at objectively, was really the executive branch accepting the limits of power put upon it by the legislative branch.

An examination of the use of military power and the federal budget shows that the system of checks and balances is not always pretty. One can even accuse it of making for a less efficient government that wavers in its direction. This wavering, however, is not a mistake; it is checks and balances creating a give-and-take that ultimately makes our democratic government responsible to those it should be responsible to: the American people.

CRITICAL COMMENTARY

This essay is a 13. It puts forth an argument that checks and balances is not always a smooth running system and then uses examples from modern history to show that the struggle between the executive and legislative branch does fulfill a premise upon which the Constitution was based.

Score: Demonstrates superiority

SECOND ESSAY FOR QUESTION TWO

The theory of checks and balances comes from Montesquieu's philosophy of divided government. He felt that not only should government be divided into various branches, but also that these branches should be interrelated so that no one branch is truly independent of the others. In this way, each branch checks or limits the powers of the other two.

America's government is divided into three branches: legislative, judicial, and executive. The president can check the judiciary through the appointment of all federal judges. The president can also check the legislature through the veto of legislation. Congress checks the judiciary by exercising its right to approve all presidential appointments. Congress can also check the president by exercising its right to override a presidential veto of legislation. The judicial branch can check both the president and legislature through its ability to declare laws and executive orders unconstitutional.

The system of checks and balances influences how our federal budget gets created. Though it is the responsibility of the president to prepare a budget every fiscal year, Congress must approve the budget. After all, the "power of the purse" is imbued in the legislative and not the executive branch. During most of the last quarter century, these two branches have been divided politically, and many presidential budgets can come to Congress "dead on arrival." Through the House of Representatives' Ways and Means Committee, many presidential budgets have been changed and amended. However, if a president does not like a budget created by Congress, he or she has a right to veto it, thus grinding government to a halt. The powers of these two branches more often than not force them to compromise, as happened with the budget agreement between Bush and Congress several years ago, which was contributed to Bush's 1992 election loss.

A second area in which the power of checks and balances comes into play is the use of the military to defend U.S. interests abroad. Though the president is the commander in chief and can send the military on police actions if he/she feels our national interests are threatened, such actions can often be checked by Congress. According to the Constitution, only Congress can declare war. Because of Vietnam, Congress passed the War Powers Act. This act allowed Congress to approve all military actions by a president. However, in 1983, the Supreme Court declared this legislative veto unconstitutional. Nevertheless, Congress can still curtail military actions by the president if they disagree with the conflict by cutting off federal funds.

CRITICAL COMMENTARY

The essay begins with a background explanation of the theory of checks and balances, describing its origin in Montesquieu's philosophy and illustrating its uses. The author then applies the theory to the federal budget and to the use of the military in defending American interests. The essay answers the presented question cogently and effectively.

Score: Demonstrates superiority

THIRD ESSAY FOR QUESTION TWO

The system of checks and balances was created in order to prevent any one person or group of persons from amassing too much power. This is achieved by requiring any action of the government to be the result of cooperation (or at least acquiescence) among all the branches of the government.

This process is perhaps most clearly demonstrated in the creation and implementation of the federal budget. The importance of checks and balances in this area is to be expected because of the role of the "power of the purse" in the evolution of the parliamentary system in our political forebear, Great Britain.

The executive branch can, and in practice does, submit a plan of what the president would like to see enacted as the budget to the legislative branch. This proposed budget has, however, no official weight. It merely informs the legislature what the president considers to be important.

The bill that eventually becomes the budget is first composed in the Ways and Means Committee in the House of Representatives. This committee has members from both parties and decides what should be passed on to be considered by the House as a whole. The House then amends and finally sends the bill to the Senate for approval. The Senate will then amend the bill and send it on to the president.

The president can either accept or reject the budget bill by signing the bill into law or vetoing it. The veto is a check on the power of the Congress. Without it there could be no review of what the Congress attempts to appropriate by taxation.

Should the president veto the bill, the bill goes back to Congress. In order to prevent the accumulation of power in the presidency to the point where one person could absolutely block the will of the representatives, a provision is made to allow for Congress to override the president's veto. But in order to avoid vitiating the president's power, both houses must vote to override by a two-thirds majority.

On the one hand, this system prevents the Congress from being excessively free with the money collected or to be collected by taxation. (Because of the pressure on every representative to "bring home the bacon" in terms of federal projects for his or her district, there is little danger of the Congress not spending enough.) At the same time, it prevents one person (the president) from dictating terms.

On the other hand, there are two dangers in this system. One is that the budget, without a guiding force, can tend to represent the internal power structure of

Washington rather than the true needs of the country. A strong president can influence Congress, as Reagan did in the early years of his presidency. Or the budget can fall prey to the amendments pushed through by the more powerful members of Congress.

The second danger is that the president and Congress can fail to see eye to eye and NO budget will pass in time. This occurs if the president is just strong enough to withstand an override attempt, but not strong enough to actually get a budget passed. The result could be as drastic as having the government close down offices for lack of funds.

Another area where checks and balances is crucial is the decision to use U.S. military power abroad. The president is the commander in chief of the armed forces, with the power and the responsibility to conduct U.S. military operations, including assigning and removing generals (as Douglas MacArthur found out in Korea). The president is allowed to send the military for noncombat police actions without the immediate approval of Congress. Thus Reagan was able to send the marines to Lebanon, and Bush could send marines to Somalia without the approval of Congress. (In the case of Somalia, Congress was not in session when the marines were sent in, and no special session was planned to give Congress a say in the matter.)

Congress alone, however, has the right to declare war. This was demonstrated during World War II when Roosevelt had to wait until the day after the attack on Pearl Harbor for Congress to issue a formal declaration.

The nature of war has changed over the years, and there are often semi-war states called police actions, such as occurred in Korea and Vietnam. Through much of the Vietnam conflict, the president had broad leeway in deciding the level of U.S. involvement. This changed with the War Powers Act, which required that the president inform Congress of any such involvement and put a limit on the length of time the troops can remain in a region without congressional approval.

The current system makes it crucial for the president to work to gain a consensus on the use of military power. This is certainly important in light of the disastrous effect of the Vietnam War on the morale of the American people.

CRITICAL COMMENTARY

This essay is comprehensive in its discussion of checks and balances. It also discusses the effects of checks and balances on the national budget and on the use of the military.

Score: Demonstrates superiority

Question Three

Political parties are one of the essential institutions in U.S government—this in spite of the fact that the Constitution makes no provisions for them. Choose ONE major political party in the United States and discuss its major distinguishing characteristics, including at least TWO of the following four topics.

(A) relationship to minority groups

(B) relationship to early U.S. politics

(C) how it has adapted to changing conditions

(D) relationship to third parties

Your essay should be a political analysis, NOT a historical survey. Be sure that you integrate your choice of topics to make a coherent essay.

ANALYSIS OF QUESTION THREE

The first choice you must make for this essay is whether to write about the Democratic or Republican party. Since the essay explicitly states that a historical survey is not what is wanted, it is advisable not to start your essay with a history of the political party; rather, it would be a good idea to state some general themes of the party that can be discussed through the essay. For example, if you wanted to argue that the Republican party has been a party that caters to business interests, you could discuss that point in the time of Lincoln, thus incorporating topic (b), and then discuss how the current Republican party has policies that appeal to business. Topic (a), minorities, is an interesting topic to discuss since the Republican party was originally the party that took an anti-slavery view stance under Lincoln's stewardship, but today the Democratic party is generally viewed as the party supporting minority interests. Topic (c), how the party has adapted to changing conditions, is the most general of the four topic choices. Once again, since a historical survey is not asked for, it is suggested that you keep to modern changes with topic (c). A good example to discuss is how either party has adapted to the age of mass media and round-the-clock news. Topic (d), third parties, can be discussed in terms of how they have influenced the major parties who have incorporated third-party ideas into their own platforms.

FIRST ESSAY FOR QUESTION THREE

In general terms, a political party is a group of citizens that share common interests—interests that would make them likely to vote for the same candidates. The Democratic party has the reputation of being the people's party, a party which has enjoyed the support of minority groups such as African Americans. This, however, was not always the case. The fact that the South has been a traditional stronghold of the Democratic party has caused historical conflicts between African Americans and the party. For years, before and up to the Civil War, the Democratic party opposed the abolition of slavery. It was a slow transformation after the Civil War that has made the Democratic party a traditional bastion of minority interests. The fact that much Republican party support came from the industrialized North, as opposed to the agrarian South, accounts for the minority support of the Democratic party. The civil rights upheaval beginning in the 1960s cemented the Democratic party's reputation as the party of African Americans. This was due partly to the strong civil rights stand taken by such Democratic leaders as John Kennedy and Lyndon Johnson.

One could say that the Democratic party exhibited flexibility in terms of Civil Rights but lacked flexibility in the 1980s, which might be one reason why they lost the presidency. Ronald Reagan brought with him new ideas that rejected many traditional "liberal" ideas of the Democratic party.

It was a period when the Democratic party seemed mired in the old way of doing things. In the 1992 election, the Democratic party showed more flexibility, campaigning on the theme of change and offering programs that many voters felt were more in touch with changes that resulted from the end of the Cold War. As party influence and the traditional role of the political parties decrease, it will be a challenge to both parties to redefine themselves and change with the times.

CRITICAL COMMENTARY

This essay is a 7 or 8. It does a good job of discussing the Democratic party's adaptability and its relationship to minority groups. It does not, however, touch on the original premise that political parties are not a result of the Constitution and could have stated a bit more on how they are essential to the government process. Even though those two topics are not the heart of the question, they were part of the question, so it is a good idea to include them in some way.

Score: Suggests competence

OUTLINE CHART FOR SECOND ESSAY

Political Party	**Characteristics**	**Relations to Minority Groups**	**Early U.S. Politics**	**Changing Conditions**	**Third Party**
Democrats	1. Party changed based on social and economic needs of the nation 2. Represented Common Man in early 19th and early 20th centuries 3. Modern philosophy of party: activist government to end business abuse, solve urban and economic problems	1. Core constituency has always been immigrants and laborers 2. Party has given political power to European immigrants, Jews, African Americans, and Hispanics	1. Jacksonian Reforms a. oppose big business b. oppose central bank c. populist	1. Lacked success when it did not adapt a. slavery 1850s–1880s b. viewed as made up of special interests not representing America 1970s–1980s	1. Adapted to change by incorporating ideas of third parties a. Greenback b. Populist c. Progressives

ANALYSIS OF THE OUTLINE CHART

The above six-column chart was used to brainstorm information needed to answer the question. Key words in the question were used to create the chart. As can be seen, only ONE political party was chosen. The second column lists its distinguishing characteristics. In creating the regular outline and the essay itself, this information can be used for comparing and contrasting either positively or negatively. The other four columns list the party's characteristics in regard to the four topics mentioned in the question. Columns could have been created for just TWO of the topics, but the writer chose to discuss the chart information on all four topics mentioned. What follows is the essay derived from the information in this chart.

SECOND ESSAY FOR QUESTION THREE

The Democratic party has survived as America's oldest political organization because of its ability to change and adapt to changing conditions. The party was at the forefront of the democratic reforms during the Jacksonian era and incorporated Progressive views during the early twentieth century. It survived and grew during the Jacksonian era by supporting the increase of the franchise and opposing big business with its stance against the creation of a central banking system. It was at this time that the party became known as representing the "common man." How the Democratic party would eventually be viewed in America became crystallized at this time. During the early twentieth century, it began to distinguish itself from the Republican party in two ways: 1) by its incorporation of the Progressive political view of activist government to end the abuses of big business, and 2) by its attempt to solve various urban problems. Because America by this time had become an urban and industrial society, the Democratic party needed to address these problems to keep the support of its core constituency: immigrants and urban workers. The party has also been viewed as the one that can solve economic problems, i.e., the New Deal, Fair Deal, and New Freedom. But in its solving of economic problems, it is perceived as never sacrificing the common or "forgotten" man.

During times when it did not adapt to changing conditions, the party tended to destroy its electability, at least on the national level. In the 1850s and 1860s it supported slavery, which contributed to a Civil War. Because of this, the party did not hold the presidency again until 1884 with the election of Grover Cleveland. A second time it did not adapt was in the 1970s and 1980s when it became perceived as no longer representing national interests. The party was viewed as being controlled by special interest groups that did not share the same values as most Americans and wanted to weaken American military.

An important strength of the Democratic party is its ability to incorporate third-party movements and turn them into constituent groups. During the nineteenth century, the Greenback movement and Populist movement were incorporated into the party, resulting in the nomination of William Jennings Bryan. In the twentieth century, constituents from the Progressive movement became incorporated into the party. Initially, these new constituents from third parties did not always lead to Democratic victories. However, they did shape the philosophy of the party and would become the core of its modern coalition, which has led to the Democrats' federal dominance in the latter twentieth century—especially in Congress. Furthermore, the party has been open to allowing new groups into its fold. It has given political power to successive immigrant groups, such as the Irish, Italians, and Jews. Presently, it is increasingly opening the process to other minorities, such as African Americans and Hispanics, as well as to women. It is this coalition that helped elect Bill Clinton president of the United States.

CRITICAL COMMENTARY

This essay begins with a brief history of the Democratic party, its inception, and its development. It discusses the party's relationship to early U.S. politics, its adaptability and lack of adaptability, and its relationship to third-party movements. The discussion of third-party movements is particularly good, as is the treatment of the Democratic party's development as a political party.

Score: Demonstrates superiority

Question Four

Government is larger and more expensive than it has ever been. Analyze the question of whether big government is beneficial or detrimental to the welfare of the country. Use TWO of the following areas.

(A) poverty and homelessness
(B) support for business
(C) the environment

In your essay discuss arguments both for and against a high degree of government involvement in people's lives. Although a brief historical perspective is permissible, the focus of the essay should be modern government

ANALYSIS OF QUESTION FOUR

As you can probably tell from the warnings against being too historical included in both this and the previous question, a common problem is that students tend to attack the questions from a historical perspective. Make sure you write the essay from the point of view of government, which means you should center it around theories about government and governmental institutions, not historical events related to government. The federal budget deficit that ballooned out of control in the 1980s has brought the question of government spending into sharper focus. Two contrasting arguments about the problems of homelessness and poverty are that on one hand, more government involvement is needed to educate and retrain disadvantaged people. Opponents to that point of view might argue that it is better for the disadvantaged to take more responsibility for their own problems, and that expanded government services and higher expenses do not necessarily solve the root problems. Investment in business in terms of research is generally seen by businesses as something positive that can increase U.S. competitiveness. Environmental protective measures are often viewed by business as government interference, but other segments of society consider them to be essential.

FIRST ESSAY FOR QUESTION FOUR

When Thomas Jefferson and James Madison were envisioning the Constitution, it is unlikely that they would have suggested the amount of government involvement in people's everyday lives that exists now. It was only after the Great Depression and the Second World War that the government became involved in people's lives to such an extent. The New Deal took hold of the economy by using government programs to employ the unemployed. The military-industrial complex that was built up during World War II never released its grip on the country and has continued to be one of the biggest government expenses.

President Johnson's Great Society program of the 1960s is an example of the government trying to solve the problems of poverty and homelessness by spending more money and thus creating a larger budget. At the time, the United States was quite prosperous, so it did not seem like a burden on the budget. The programs obviously did a lot of good for a lot of people, but it was expensive. When the economy got worse, people started complaining about the mismanagement of the government budget.

The Vietnam War is an example of where the government had to spend a lot of money to win a war. In situations like that, the government has no choice and must spend, then think of a way to pay for it. Wars can also stimulate the economy by giving people jobs. The problem is how should the jobs be paid for?

Now we have a budget deficit. The Congress has been spending more money than the government has been raising. Different politicians have different theories on how to help the economy. Some say cleaning the environment will hurt the economy. Others say that environmental technology can make money. Overall, the government tries to find a balance between spending too much and investing too little.

CRITICAL COMMENTARY

This is a weak essay, probably a 3 or 4 at the highest. It suffers from the classic problem of listing historical examples without any clear thesis or development. The first paragraph has some promise, but the promise is never fulfilled. There is no sophistication in the ideas, and the essay never explores the key to the question: What are the theories behind government spending and growth?

Score: Suggests incompetence

SECOND ESSAY FOR QUESTION FOUR

Many believe that big government can protect the environment and end homelessness as well as poverty. Those in favor of government intervention cite the fact that homelessness has grown in the 1980s because of the curtailment of the federal government's safety net. In the Reagan years, federally subsidized housing programs were ended and many anti-poverty programs were cut, such as Aid to Dependent Children and food stamps. Concomitantly, many states initiated deinstitutionalization when federal funds were cut for halfway houses and group homes—especially in urban centers. On the other hand, those who are against big government feel that programs such as these foster dependency. They feel most people who are homeless willfully choose this lifestyle and do not want to be helped. Conservatives feel the homeless are being used for nefarious political purposes. If the homeless can organize to protect their right to sleep in subway stations, why can't they organize themselves to get out of their predicament? Conservatives are against all anti-poverty programs. They interpret the Constitution strictly and feel the federal government has no responsibility to insure economic equality in any way. Any programs to help the poor should be limited to charity and/or the states.

Most of those who favor big government feel that federal power must be used to curtail pollution and protect wilderness areas. Environmentalists feel there should be strict government regulation of business to prohibit them from polluting the atmosphere and earth with toxic waste. They feel farmers must be prevented from using certain insecticides that can possibly cause cancer. More land should be protected to prevent industrial development. More animals should be protected to prevent extinction. Polluted areas should be cleaned up and reclaimed. Our wilderness areas should be kept in their pristine state. Those against big government feel such regulation will curtail economic expansion in a time when our economy is still sluggish. It will cost businesses more money to comply with these regulations, and the cost will be passed on to the consumer. They feel market forces are the best means to protect the environment. Businesses will not pollute if it is not profitable to do so. On the other hand, environmentalists feel that investing in environmental protection will create more jobs. Furthermore, if taxes have to be raised or the price of goods are increased because of environmental regulations, it is a price well paid to protect our natural resources for future generations.

CRITICAL COMMENTARY

This essay addresses the issue of large government in relation to homelessness and the environment. The discussion of homelessness gives arguments both pro and con to federal intervention. Similarly, the author presents arguments both for and against environmental regulations.

Score: Demonstrates superiority

THIRD ESSAY FOR QUESTION FOUR

A well-known joke asks for the definition of an elephant. The answer is that an elephant is a mouse built to government specifications. As with many jokes, there is an underlying layer of truth in the situation described. Government is powerful enough to make an elephant, but often not sensitive enough to build a mouse when appropriate.

The tragic problem of poverty in this country has provoked the government to look for some way to redistribute the wealth so that suffering can be alleviated. But at the same time, government has had to take into account the fact that its ability to help is based on its tax base, and that therefore the government must support those from whom it is seeking to redistribute wealth.

This results in the need for a balancing act. Those steps that promote social and economic growth will point towards the positive value of an active government. Those that overstep the bounds will point to the necessity of realizing that government cannot do everything.

Welfare is one of the most divisive issues in terms of both cost and rationale. There are those who view welfare as a positive process that stimulates the economy in the short run by injecting money into the system that would not otherwise be there; in the long run people not crushed by poverty will be more likely to become productive.

Others see welfare as presently constituted as a way of promoting and perpetuating failure by separating a person's acts from the consequences of the acts.

There is truth in both positions. But the answer can hardly be simply to cut back welfare. Regulations have to be drawn up that allow people to have some input into their lives, but not to promote an attitude of immunity to disaster.

For example, welfare rules should not immediately deduct a dollar in benefits for every dollar earned. What such a rule does is give the recipient no incentive to work at all.

When dealing with business, the government has a responsibility to provide a stable environment for business to operate. It also has a responsibility as the advocate of last resort for the consumers that are the constituency of the government. *Caveat emptor* is valid only when the resources of providers and receivers of goods and services are roughly equal.

Government cannot overregulate business; otherwise it fails to protect our tax and job base and infrastructure. Neither can it allow business to fleece consumers. The question is not whether to regulate, but how best to do so.

Banks, for example, were regulated after the disaster of 1929. Reagan selectively deregulated the savings and loans while leaving the bailout mechanism in place. The result is a fiasco we will pay for years.

CRITICAL COMMENTARY

The writer answers the question well, providing arguments both pro and con to government involvement in people's lives. The treatment of poverty is excellent. The treatment of business is good.

Score: Demonstrates superiority

Chapter 3

The Practice Stimulus-Based Free-Response Question

The stimulus-based free-response question tests your ability to create and justify a response to a question using data that is presented to you. The data may be in the form of charts, graphs, quotations, excerpts from books, etc.

This question is meant to assess your ability to interpret and analyze information given in light of your knowledge of U.S. government. Therefore, stay away from mere paraphrasing, repetition, or summary of information; instead, focus on interpretation, analysis of material, and supporting a conclusion.

Here are six stimulus-based free-response questions and approaches to answering each one. Before you read the answers, try each question on your own and see how it compares with the suggested approach.

Question One

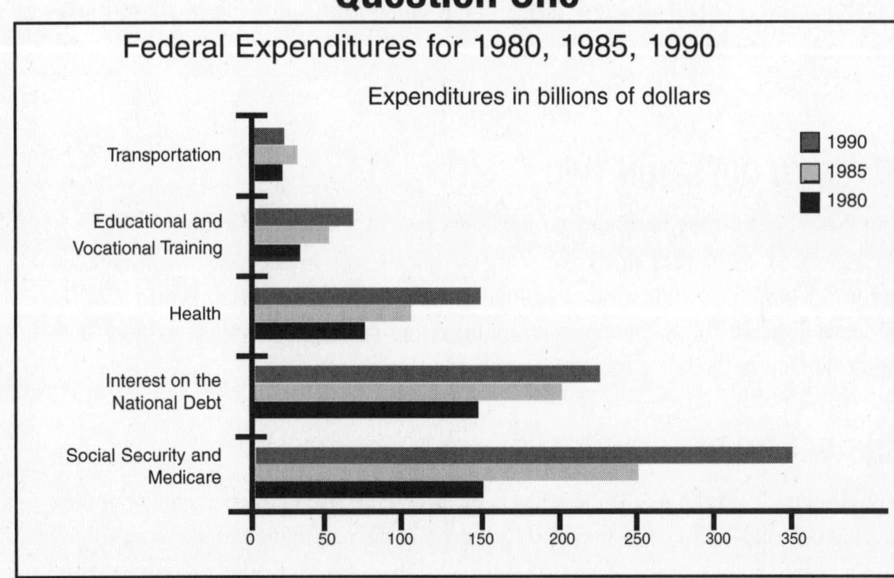

Using the data in the graph above, answer two of the following questions.

(A) What is the major cause for sharp raises in federal expenditures?

(B) How much money would be saved by eliminating entitlement programs in 1990?

(C) What information supplied points to serious fiscal problems?

ANSWER TO QUESTION ONE

(A) There is a correlation between major wars and an increase in expenditures.

(B) Entitlement programs are programs that give benefits to all qualified persons. Eliminating the programs would save $345 billion.

(C) The steady increase in federal expenditures is significant. The most significant factor is that paying interest (not principal) on the debt is the country's third highest expenditure.

Question Two

Employment Trends

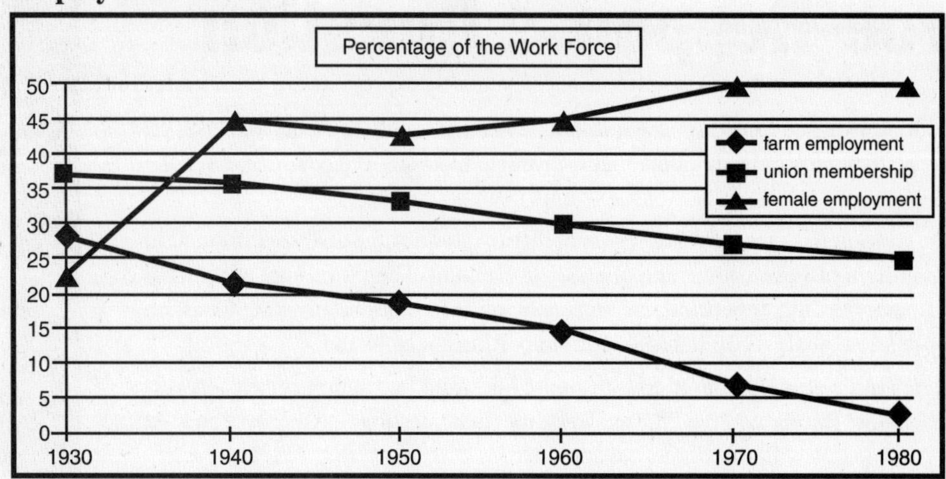

Using the graph above and your knowledge of government, answer the following two questions.

(A) What three trends are identified in this graph?

(B) Is there a connection between the three trends? Explain.

FIRST ANSWER TO QUESTION TWO

(A) Decrease in farmers, decrease in unionized jobs, increase in employed women.

(B) The trends are related. A change to a service economy might explain a decrease in unionized and agricultural jobs. The introduction of women into the labor force during World War II and the increased desire for independence among American women might explain the steady rise of women in the labor force after 1945.

SECOND ANSWER TO QUESTION TWO

(A) Since the beginning of World War II there has been an overall rise in the percentage of the work force that is female. There has been a steady drop in the percentage of the work force that belongs to a union, and a tremendous drop in the number of farm workers relative to the total labor force.

(B) An argument can be made for a connection of these three trends if two key assumptions are made. If we assume that women generally work in service jobs, and that service providers do not unionize, then the drop in percentages of both union membership and farm labor is due to the increase in female employment. To verify this, we would need to see if the numbers of workers in manufacturing and farming remained the same while the total labor force grew.

Question Three

"... By the report before us, we propose to annihilate, at one stroke, all those property distinctions and to bow before the idol of universal suffrage. That extreme democratic principle, when applied to the legislative and executive departments of government, has been regarded with terror by the wise men of every age because, in every European republic, ancient and modern, in which it has been tried, it has terminated disastrously and been productive of corruption, injustice, violence, and tyranny, and dare we flatter ourselves that we are a peculiar people who can run the career of history, exempted from the passions which have disturbed and corrupted the best of mankind? If we are like other races of men, with similar follies and vices, then I greatly fear that our posterity will have reason to deplore, in sackcloth and ashes, the delusion of the day...

Now, sir, I wish to preserve our senate as the representative of the landed interest. I wish those who have an interest in the soil to retain the exclusive ownership and rights in which they may find safety through all the vicissitudes which the state may be destined, in the course of Providence, to experience. I wish them to be always enabled to say that their freeholds cannot be taxed without their consent..."

Answer the following questions based on the above reading passage.

(A) What is the writer arguing against?

(B) What are two reasons the author uses to support his argument, and what argument might you use to rebut him?

FIRST ANSWER TO QUESTION THREE

(A) He is arguing against letting people other than his fellow landowners join the Senate.

(B) He argues that history has shown "extreme democracy" to be a mistake, and that only people who own land should be in charge of property taxes. There are many arguments that could be used to rebut him, including the basic principle upon which our nation was founded: All men are created equal.

SECOND ANSWER TO QUESTION THREE

(A) The author is arguing against the Seventeenth Amendment of the Constitution, which allowed for the direct election of senators. Previously, senators were picked by the state legislatures, which generally consisted of the "landed interests" because they were the ones who could afford to run for office.

(B) The author maintains that the landed classes pay the most in taxes and therefore are entitled to special representation. He also argues that history is littered with the corpses of states who died of the tyranny of the "great unwashed."

Tyranny, however, more often wears the crown of special interest than the liberty cap of the sans-culotte of the French Revolution. Plutocracy is not notorious for its benevolence.

Question Four

State Tax Bills Sent by Congress for 1786

State	Tax Bill	Amount Paid by June 30, 1786	Balance Due
New Hampshire	$186,799	$7,679	$179,119
Massachusetts	653,798	371,118	282,679
Rhode Island	108,342	75,711	32,630
Connecticut	373,598	157,318	216,279
New York	186,799	186,799	–
New Jersey	242,839	139,328	103,510
Pennsylvania	560,379	560,379	–
Delaware	56,042	29,081	26,961
Maryland	466,998	272,525	194,472
Virginia	653,797	550,849	102,947
North Carolina	311,338	–	311,338
South Carolina	186,799	186,799	–
Georgia	12,452	–	12,452

Using the above chart and your knowledge of United States politics, answer the following two questions.

(A) What two states would likely express the strongest reservations about the revenue collection system used in the Articles of Confederation?

(B) Explain the problem illustrated by this chart and the eventual solution.

ANSWER TO QUESTION FOUR

(A) North Carolina and Georgia did not even attempt to pay the amount owed to the national government in taxes. This suggests that either they could not afford to or were protesting the collection in principle.

(B) This inefficient and unenforceable method of collecting taxes for the national government was eventually replaced when, in the Constitution, the national government was given the right to levy taxes independent of the states.

Question Five

Three views on the role of the president:

(I) It is my opinion that a president should empower the government to find solutions to our economic and social problems. He or she must guarantee equal opportunity for all American citizens regardless of race, creed, sex, or sexual orientation. All Americans should be guaranteed a decent education from preschool through college. Higher education should be provided at minimal cost to all citizens. A president must propose laws that will ensure that all Americans will not be subject to the harsh whims of the marketplace. Job training must be provided for all unemployed Americans in skills that will be needed in the twenty-first century. A decent wage should be guaranteed as well as universal health care. Legislation should be proposed that will guarantee that the elderly, infirm, and physically and mentally handicapped are treated with dignity. Decent housing and a minimum income should be provided for all. To pay for all these needs, the income tax needs to be more progressive. It is the obligation of the rich to pay for society's needs. In addition, by guaranteeing a decent income for all Americans, consumers will be able to buy more goods, thus increasing economic activity as well as the tax base to pay for all these needed programs.

(II) I feel that whenever the federal government tries to solve an economic or social problem, not only is the problem aggravated, but we also tend to lose a little more of our basic freedom. The basic role of a president should be to provide for our common defense and allow the marketplace to solve our problems. There is no right to universal health care, a living wage, or a decent education. If government keeps its hands off, all these issues will be resolved. The president cannot pass laws to guarantee equal results. In any market economy, some people will succeed and some will fail. An employer has the right not to hire someone who will not benefit the company economically. I want a president that will end most government regulations on industry and commerce. In this way, economic growth will spur forward. Without an excessive federal bureaucracy, taxes will be reduced, thus increasing the buying power as well as the paycheck of most Americans.

(III) I want a president that will focus on the national interests of this country. If our interests are jeopardized abroad, the president should not be afraid to use force if necessary to protect Americans or American property. However, we should not be the policemen of the world. Any president who would get involved in a third-world war would face the wrath of the American people. Coffee or sugar is no reason to risk American lives. Also, we need a president who will ensure that we remain prosperous economically. This person should keep his/her hands off when the GNP is growing, but be able to harness our national energy when times are bad. There is nothing wrong with providing a tax cut and creating public works projects to spur employment. We need laws to improve education, but not to tell us who to go to school with. Yes, a good president has to tackle important national issues, such as skyrocketing health care. However, we must remain free to choose our own doctors and hospitals. Furthermore, we need a president who is fiscally responsible. The debt has to be controlled, so that entitlements such as social security and workmen's compensation will not be threatened. The president must have the leadership necessary to tackle special interests in order to cut bureaucratic waste and the welfare benefits of the undeserving. Laws must be proposed so that only those truly in need will get a handout.

Using the three quotes above and your knowledge of U.S. government and politics, perform the following two tasks:

(A) Name two political issues pertaining to the role of the president that the three citizens would likely agree upon based on the explicit or implicit ideas they expressed.

(B) Discuss which of the three citizens would most likely support a president who favors school vouchers and opposes a gasoline tax. Give at least three reasons to support your answer.

ANSWER TO QUESTION FIVE

(A) All three would most likely support a president who decided to use troops to protect vital national interests abroad. Speaker I wants to guarantee America's prosperity. Therefore, if the export of Middle East oil was threatened and American jobs could be affected, Speaker I would probably support a limited military action. Speaker II explicitly states that the government must provide for national defense and maintains property rights are of vital importance. Therefore, if American property is threatened abroad, we must intervene. Speaker III also explicitly says that the president has the right to use military force to protect American interests.

All three may be pro-choice with regard to abortion. Speaker I approves of government interference in economic, but not social, matters—for example, supporting equal rights regardless of sexual orientation. Speaker I would not want the government to interfere with a woman's right to an abortion. Speaker II seems to be a true conservative, saying that the marketplace will solve all economic and "social" issues. It would be hypocritical for Speaker II to favor the government limiting abortion rights. The executive would need to implement many government regulations to police such a curb, and Speaker II wants an executive branch with limited abilities to interfere only when necessary. This moderate point of view seems to favor the government interfering economically but not socially. Speaker III does not want the government to dictate which children shall attend a particular school or which doctor a person should consult. Thus, we can infer that Speaker III would probably not want the government to tell women whether they should or should not have an abortion.

(B) The best choice is Speaker III. Speaker II wants a limited government and would want to cut the gasoline tax. Indeed, Speaker II believes the executive branch should not propose or implement such a tax in the first place. Speaker II would probably not even support an income tax. The most Speaker II would probably allow would be those taxes explicitly allowed by the federal government in the Constitution (tariffs and excise taxes). However, Speaker II would definitely not favor school vouchers. Though Speaker II favors school choice, vouchers assume redistributing income from one group to another. Speaker II would say that the government would get this income through taxation, which Speaker II opposes. Speaker II would probably prefer that such a system of vouchers be left to the state or local government. After all, nowhere in the Constitution is it mentioned that the federal government or executive branch has a role to play in terms of public or private education.

Lastly, Speaker I, who wants increased taxes and direct federal spending on education, is not even to be considered. On the other hand, Speaker III is the most logical choice. Speaker III supports federal aid to education but does not want the government to dictate which children shall attend a particular school. The voucher system is the logical answer to the problem. Speaker III would accept federal money to pay for sending a child to a selected public or private school. Speaker III would also oppose a gasoline tax, believing that if anything, the government should provide tax cuts rather than tax increases—especially if the economy goes sour. Speaker III believes that if the government needs money to pay for necessary programs, the fiscal resources can be found by cutting government spending in other areas.

Question Six

Andrew Jackson's Views on the Bank of the United States
(excerpts from his 1832 message)

"A bank of the United States is in many respects convenient for the Government and useful to the people. Entertaining this opinion, and deeply impressed with the belief that some of the powers and privileges possessed by the existing bank are unauthorized by the Constitution, subversive of the rights of the States, and dangerous to the liberties of the people, I felt it my duty...to call the attention of Congress to the practicability of organizing an institution combining all its advantages and obviating these objections.

But this act does not permit competition in the purchase of this monopoly. It seems to be predicated on the erroneous idea that the present stock holders have...rights...to the bounty of Government. It appears that more than a fourth part of the stock is held by foreigners and the residue is held by a few hundred of our own citizens, chiefly of the richest class. For their benefit does this act exclude the whole American people from competition in the purchase of this monopoly and dispose of it for many millions less than it is worth.

In another of its bearings this provision is fraught with danger. Of the 25 directors of this bank, five are chosen by the Government and 20 by the citizen stockholders. From all voice in these elections, the foreign stockholders are excluded by the charter. In proportion, therefore, as the stock is transferred to foreign holders the extent of suffrage in the choice of directors is curtailed...Should the stock of the bank principally pass into the hands of the subjects of a foreign country and we should unfortunately become involved in a war with that country, what would be our condition?"

Using the above excerpt and your knowledge of U.S. politics, perform the following two tasks:

(A) Identify two of President Jackson's viewpoints that could be categorized as populist.

(B) Give one possible counterargument that a member of the Congress could use to debate Jackson.

FIRST ANSWER TO QUESTION SIX

(A) Populism, which is most similar to modern liberalism as a political philosophy, had a rural base and opposed business domination of U.S. politics. It favored greater government regulation and an easy monetary policy. Fear of monopoly and rule by an elite group of the richest citizens would be in line with populist politics. Jackson also states that some privileges possessed by the existing bank are subversive to the rights of states.

(B) An opponent of Jackson's views on the Bank of the United States could say that his concerns about control of the bank and a war with the country that holds a large share of the stock are contrived, since these are things that could easily be monitored and regulated as necessary. A person might also argue that there is nothing wrong with citizens profiting from "the bounty of Government."

SECOND ANSWER TO QUESTION SIX

(A) The populist creed is that democracy is the right of the many to be protected from the incursions of the few. Jackson points to a number of problems that the populist would have with a Bank of the United States. Two of these problems ultimately rest on the concentration of power in the hands of a few not chosen by the many.

First of all, the bank is to be run by the stockholders, all of whom presumably are rich, and none of whom have any qualifications other than being rich and holding stock.

Secondly, while stock can be bought by anyone, only citizen stockholders can vote. To the extent that the stock is in the hands of foreigners, the power of the citizen stockholders is further concentrated.

(B) It could be pointed out that the bank will have government representatives on it, and that the bank will certainly be subject to scrutiny by Congress at periodic intervals. The fact that the stockholders are rich merely means that they are good at managing money, and it is pointless to deprive the American citizens of their expertise.

PART 2

THE REVIEW OF U.S. GOVERNMENT AND POLITICS

PREVIEW

THE REVIEW OF U.S. GOVERNMENT AND POLITICS

This chapter provides a review of the major topics in U.S. government and politics that are covered on the Advanced Placement examination. The topics are divided as follows:

A. Origins of the Constitution
B. Content and Structure of the Constitution
C. The Legislative Branch
D. The Executive Branch
E. The Judicial Branch
F. Bureaucracy
G. Political Parties
H. Elections
I. Political Socialization
J. Interest Groups and Lobbying
K. Civil Liberties and Civil Rights

How This Review Is Organized

Each unit of the government review is divided into five sections:

1. **Major Themes and Questions**
   In this section, several broad questions of analysis are posed that suggest some of the major issues of the unit.
2. **Major Terms and Concepts**
   This section is a list of important names, places, ideas, and events that fall within the time frame of the unit.
3. **Sample Outline**
   This section provides outlines of answers to questions of analysis. Some are designed to answer very broad questions; others deal with much narrower aspects of the period involved.
4. **Chronology**
   This section organizes the unit in correct time sequence. The AP U.S. Government and Politics exam often asks the students to put events into their proper, chronological order.
5. **Short Reading List**
   This section includes major works of interpretation and some classic sources, e.g., Locke's *The Second Treatise of Government* and Hobbes's *Leviathan*. It may also list a few works of fiction that give a sense of the period (or at least the author's notion of the period). You may need to be familiar with generally recognized literature in the field.

None of these review chapters is designed to replace an actual text of U.S. government. They are based on a learning theory, which stresses reinforcement of previously learned material. They cannot be used without reference to your own AP course. They do, however, recall and suggest information useful for the examination.

Chapter

Origins of the Constitution

MAJOR THEMES AND QUESTIONS

Early Philosophical Influences

1. Describe the importance of the philosophies of the Enlightenment and the theory of natural rights to the framing of the Constitution.
2. What basic elements do all governments have in common?
3. What early contributions did Greece and Rome make to democracy?
4. Compare the Athenian Assembly to our modern democratic institutions.
5. What criticisms of democracy did Plato write about in the *Republic*?
6. What did Jefferson mean when he said his duty was not to announce "new principles...never before thought," but instead to "place before making the common sense of the subject..."?
7. How did the English jurist Sir Edward Coke's ideas that the actions of Parliament had to conform to "common right and reason" eventually take root in America?

Historical Setting

1. What were the different types of governments and institutions that existed in early American colonies?
2. What British legislative acts led to the Revolution?
3. What did the First and Second Continental Congresses accomplish?
4. How were the Albany Plan of Union, Stamp Act Congress, Committees of Correspondence, Sons of Liberty, Nonintercouse Agreements, etc., early experiments with the Union?
5. What were some inconsistencies between the ideas expressed in the Declaration of Independence and the realities of eighteenth-century America?
6. How was the rebellious atmosphere of eighteenth-century America both a catalyst and an impediment to the forming of a union?
7. Describe to what extent America's early colonial governments were based on the British system.

Articles of Confederation

1. What financial and economic problems caused leaders to want a Second Continental Congress?
2. In what ways did the Articles of Confederation give more power to the Republic?
3. How did equal representation for the states make for unequal representation for the people?
4. How did the confederation protect individual states from being taken over by foreign countries?
5. What were the flaws of the Articles of Confederation?

Philadelphia Convention

1. What was the impetus for the meeting in 1787 to revise the Articles of Confederation?
2. Why did some states and delegates refuse to attend the convention?
3. Describe the organization and running of the convention?
4. What caused convention members to create a constitution based on federalism?
5. Describe the three major compromises that were reached.
6. Why is Madison considered the "Father of the Constitution"?
7. Was it an accident of history that such a group of talented thinkers assembled to create the Constitution?
8. What were the contributions of different members? (55 delegates)
9. How could slavery be reconciled with the basic philosophy behind the Constitution?
10. Compare the political and economic concerns at the convention.

Steps Toward Ratification

1. Who led the Federalists and Antifederalists? What were their opposing positions?
2. What local concerns of delegates from different states caused debate over the Constitution's ratification?
3. Why did Patrick Henry say, "I look upon that paper as the most fatal plan that could possibly be conceived to enslave a free people" in reference to the not-yet-ratified Constitution?
4. Why did Federalists promise a Bill of Rights when the Constitution was ratified?
5. What states voted to ratify the Constitution, and why?
6. How did the media, specifically the *Federalist Papers*, sway public opinion?

MAJOR TERMS AND CONCEPTS

People

John Locke, philosopher
Voltaire, philosopher
Montesquieu, philosopher
Rousseau, philosopher
George Washington
Patrick Henry, Antifederalist
John Hancock, Antifederalist
Samuel Adams, Antifederalist
William Samuel Johnson
Thomas Jefferson
John Dickinson
Gouverneur Morris
James Madison, "Father of the Constitution"
Benjamin Franklin
Alexander Hamilton
Oliver Ellsworth
Thomas Hobbes, philosopher

Early Influences

Magna Carta
Glorious Revolution
Second Treatise on Civil Government
Federalist Papers
Albany Plan
Committees of Correspondence
Declaration of Rights and Grievances
Enlightenment
social contract theory
Treaty of Paris
Athenian democracy
Roman law
Declaration of Independence
Articles of Confederation
Mayflower Compact
Stamp Act Congress
Sons of Liberty
nonintercourse
First Continental Congress
Second Continental Congress
Common Law
doctrine of natural rights
Spirit of the Laws

General Government Terms

anarchy
totalitarianism
feudalism
democracy
direct democracy
federal government
monarchy
capitalism
confederation
constitutionalism
republic
indirect democracy
laissez faire
proletariat
representative democracy
socialism
unitary government
social contract
antifederalism
tyrant
prime minister
tyranny of the majority
nation
oligarchy
sovereignty
state
bureaucracy
fascism
Parliament
premier

Articles of Confederation

national legislative body
government for common defense
Northwest Ordinance of 1785
unanimous vote for amendments
state autonomy
one vote per state
Congress of Confederation
Land Ordinance of 1785
continental currency, no value
Shays's Rebellion
Annapolis Convention

Constitutional Convention

Philadelphia, 1787	Federalists
bicameral legislature	unicameral legislature
Virginia Plan	interstate commerce
slavery compromise	New Jersey Plan
Connecticut Compromise	three-fifths compromise
Great Compromise	conventions, nine states
ratification	Antifederalists

SAMPLE OUTLINE

To what extent did economic factors influence the framers of the Constitution? To properly discuss this question, several areas must be explored. What was the economic background of the delegates and the people they represented? What parts of the Constitution that were debated and/or included in the final document had economic ramifications? It would be interesting to discuss whether economic considerations had a positive or negative effect on the final product. The question could also be discussed in terms of whether the Constitution is still effective for our modern economy, which is much different from the one that existed when the Constitution was framed.

ECONOMIC CONSIDERATIONS AND THE FRAMING OF THE CONSTITUTION

I. Economic impetus for the Constitution

- A. The meaning of freedom in the Constitution
  1. Laissez faire
  2. People free to improve their material existences
  3. Government cannot compel people toward any particular vocation
- B. Economic motives behind the American Revolution
  1. Taxation without representation
  2. Resentment of British mercantile goals
- C. Constitutional Convention called to deal with interstate commerce problems

II. Economic issues addressed in the Constitution

- A. Interstate commerce
  1. Southern states feared North would cut off cotton trade
  2. Compromise gave central government power to regulate interstate commerce
  3. Taxation of exports was forbidden
- B. Slavery was preserved for economic reasons
  1. Congress prohibited from interfering with slave trade until at least 1808
  2. Each slave counted as three-fifths of a person
  3. Provisions for slavery nullified in 1865 by Thirteenth Amendment

III. Delegates and self-interest

A. Argument 1: The Constitution benefited the interests of a few

1. Benefits for "personality" interests

a. Finance

b. Trade

c. Manufacturing

2. Lack of benefits for "realty" interests

a. Landowners

b. Debtors

c. Farmers

B. Argument 2: Different classes were represented by the framers of the Constitution.

1. Interests of northern states

a. Manufacturing

b. Importing cheap goods

2. Interests of southern states

a. Cotton exports

b. Cheap slave labor

C. Argument 3: The Constitution was more political than economic

1. Denies state primary control in key areas

a. Currency

b. Commerce

c. Contracts

2. Removed sources of contention between states

3. The kind of political development that framers considered healthy was encouraged in the Constitution

a. Enhanced protection for commerce and creditors

b. Power to tax

IV. Constitution is flexible enough to deal with a variety of interests

CHRONOLOGY

The Road to a Constitution

1619 **House of Burgesses** is established in Virginia, constituting America's first representative assembly.

1620 **Mayflower Compact** sets up a governing system for the Plymouth colonists.

1639 **Fundamental Orders of Connecticut** are adopted, representing America's first written constitution.

1643 **New England Confederation** is organized; New England colonies cooperate to combat native American peoples.

1754 **Albany Plan of Union** proposes a colonial confederation, but colonists reject it.

1765 **Stamp Act Congress** petitions and forces repeal of the British Stamp Act; unifies boycott by colonies.

1770 **Committees of Correspondence** unifies resistance to British policies.

1774 **First Continental Congress** is held; 12 colonies meet to petition the king to repeal "Intolerable Acts" and to organize a boycott.

1775 **Second Continental Congress** provides a government for the colonies during the Revolution.

1776 **Declaration of Independence** declares separation of the colonies from Britain.

1781 **Articles of Confederation** are adopted as the first national constitution.

1783 **Treaty of Paris** ends the revolutionary war.

1787 **Constitutional Convention** results in the writing of a new constitution.

1788 **Constitution ratified by nine states**, the number necessary to bring the Constitution into legal existence.

SHORT READING LIST

Edward Conrad Smith, ed., *The Constitution of the United States*, 11th ed. Gives a comprehensive and straightforward overview of the Constitution and its origins, as well as important documents that led up to it. Also includes selected Supreme Court cases summarized and grouped according to topic.

William Anderson, *The Nation and the States: Rivals or Partners?* Discusses the question of federalism from a historical and a modern perspective. Also discusses the dynamics of the central and local competition for political and economic power.

Charles A. Beard, *An Economic Interpretation of the Constitution;* and Robert E. Brown, *Charles Beard and the Constitution*. These works give opposing views to the debate over the extent to which the Constitution was written for the economic benefit of a certain group.

Catherine Drinker Bowen, *Miracle at Philadelphia*. Creates a vivid picture of the personalities and issues that struggled against each other during the process of writing and ratifying the Constitution. It clearly describes the serendipitous way many essential aspects of the Constitution came to be included.

Edward F. Cooke, *A Detailed Analysis of the Constitution*. Gives a thorough analysis of the components of the Constitution and discusses how the Constitution has been applied to the running of the government.

Jonathan Elliot, ed., *The Debates in the Several State Conventions on the Adoption of the Federal Constitution as Recommended by the General Convention in Philadelphia in 1787*. Gives a good description of the debate over federalism and antifederalism as argued prior to the Constitution's ratification, as well as an in-depth view of regional interests at the time.

Robert A. Dahl, *A Preface to Democratic Theory*. This discussion of democratic theories helps to put U.S. democracy in the overall context of general theories on representative governments.

Thomas Hobbes, *Leviathan*; John Locke, *The Second Treatise of Government*; and John Stuart Mill, *On Liberty*. These three classic texts provide a historical and philosophical setting as well as insight into influences on the creators of the Constitution.

Chapter 5

Content and Structure of the Constitution

MAJOR THEMES AND QUESTIONS

Principles of the Constitution

1. How does the Preamble of the Constitution express in a simple manner the principles behind the Constitution?
2. How did the Constitution allocate powers according to the system of federalism?
3. How did the Constitution set up a system of checks and balances?
4. What is the relation between the Enlightenment and the system of checks and balances?
5. Describe the articles of the Constitution that deal with the federal–state relationship.
6. What concept of justice was established by the Constitution?
7. In what way does the Constitution "provide for the common defense"?
8. Why has the term *majestic vagueness* been used to describe the Constitution?
9. Discuss the terms *popular sovereignty* and *representative democracy* in reference to the Constitution.
10. How does the Constitution insure popular sovereignty?
11. Explain the importance of elasticity and how the Constitution made provisions for expansion and change.
12. How close has the United States come to the ideals set forth in the Preamble?
13. Describe what the framers of the Constitution meant by a secular system of government.
14. What is the relationship between the philosophies set down in the Declaration of Independence and the Constitution?
15. What is liberty and why is it a difficult concept to define and guarantee for all people?
16. To what extent does the phrase "a more perfect Union" from the Preamble equivocate with regard to one of the Constitution's goals? Why do you think the framers of the Constitution did not state this goal more emphatically?
17. What is the significance of "fundamental law" in terms of the Constitution?
18. What is the importance of brevity in the Constitution? Why do you think it was written with fewer than 6,000 words?

ROAD MAP

First Seven Articles of the Constitution

1. What parameters does Article One of the Constitution create for the legislative branch of government?
2. Why and how were portions of Section 3 and Section 4 of Article One of the Constitution changed?
3. What differences were established in houses of the bicameral legislature?
4. Why were portions of Article Two, Section 1; Article Three, Section 2; and Article Four, Section 2 of the Constitution changed?
5. Describe how Article Four of the Constitution sets forth the rights of states.
6. Describe the importance of the "elastic clause" to the Constitution and its adaptability to new circumstances as they arise.
7. What part of Article Six points out the secular nature of the Constitution?

Bill of Rights

1. Why was it necessary to agree to the Bill of Rights before the Constitution was ratified?
2. What English and colonial experiences led to the Bill of Rights?
3. What elements of a secular government are found in the First Amendment?
4. Give examples of the freedoms guaranteed by the First Amendment.
5. What were the historical concerns that brought about the Second and Third Amendments?
6. Discuss the current debate over the Second Amendment's guaranteed right to bear arms in terms of the NRA's stance, as well as the stance of the people advocating stricter gun control.
7. Are the Second and Third Amendments anachronisms? Discuss whether they are relevant to modern times.
8. What do the Fourth through Eighth Amendments say about life, liberty, and property?
9. Discuss how the Fourth through Eighth Amendments are relevant to current concerns over victims' rights.
10. Which amendment would be cited by someone who does not wish to discuss his/her involvement in a criminal trial?
11. Does the Fourth Amendment eliminate all search and seizure? How does the word "unreasonable" leave room for differences of interpretation?
12. What is meant by "cruel and unusual" in the Eighth Amendment? How has that term been interpreted?
13. What are the purposes of the Ninth and Tenth Amendments?

Later Amendments

1. By what procedures can the Constitution be amended?
2. How does the Eleventh Amendment change Article Three?
3. What historical event brought on the Twelfth Amendment?
4. Why were electors given one vote instead of two in the Twelfth Amendment?
5. Describe the relationship between the growth of political parties and the Twelfth Amendment.
6. What part of the Twelfth Amendment was later changed by the Twentieth Amendment?
7. Describe the "Civil War amendments."
8. What is the relationship between the Thirteenth Amendment and Lincoln's Emancipation Proclamation?
9. What part of the Fourteenth Amendment was worded to punish Confederate states?
10. Describe how the court case beginning with *Gitlow v. New York* (1925) expanded the due process protection put into the Fourteenth Amendment to help former slaves.
11. How did southern states find ways of avoiding the political rights for minorities set forth in the Fifteenth Amendment?
12. Did the Sixteenth Amendment diminish state rights?
13. How did the Sixteenth Amendment override *Pollock v. Farmer's Loan & Trust Co.*?
14. How did the Seventeenth Amendment make elections for senators more democratic?
15. Describe the historical context that helped to create the Eighteenth Amendment, but also made it difficult to enforce.
16. What was the relationship between the Eighteenth and Twenty-first Amendments?
17. Describe the significance of the Nineteenth Amendment to the struggle for women's rights.
18. How did the Twentieth Amendment improve the problem of having a "lame duck" president?
19. In what way did the Twenty-first Amendment support states' rights?
20. What historical event led to the Twenty-second Amendment?
21. How did the Twenty-third Amendment increase the rights of people living in the District of Columbia?
22. In what way did the Twenty-fourth Amendment improve minority rights?
23. Describe the relationship between the Twenty-fourth Amendment and *Harper v. Virginia State Board of Elections* (1966).
24. In what way did the Twenty-fifth Amendment create stability in case of presidential illness?
25. What is the relationship between *Oregon v. Mitchell* (1970) and the Twenty-sixth Amendment?

MAJOR TERMS AND CONCEPTS

Ideas Behind the Constitution

popular sovereignty
Bill of Rights
constitutional amendment
religious test
executive power
judicial power
legislative power
confederation
checks and balances
bill of attainder
due process of law
separation of powers
extradition
full faith and credit clause
federation
political legitimacy
power of the purse
privileges and immunities clause
elasticity
selective incorporation of the Bill of Rights
rule of law
tyranny of the majority
unitary government
constituency
Preamble
brevity

Phrases Used in the Constitution

justice
general welfare
impeachment
treason
emoluments
duties
imposts
naturalization
militia
habeas corpus
all intents and purposes
abridging freedom
domestic tranquility
pro tempore
quorum
breach of peace
collect taxes
excise
regulate commerce
letters of marque and reprisal
arsenals
ex post facto
jurisdiction
suffrage
common law
speedy and public trial
impartial jury
slavery
insurrection and rebellion
prohibition
unreasonable searches and seizures
involuntary servitude
apportionment
census or enumeration
poll tax

SAMPLE OUTLINE

The lofty goal of securing the "blessings of liberty" has not always been simple to obtain. How has the term liberty changed and developed? What parts of the Constitution deal with the difficult task of securing liberty? What has liberty meant to Americans? Has there always been a consensus on what types of liberty are important and to what extent liberty has to be guaranteed? When does one person's or group's liberty infringe on the rights of others? These are some of the issues that could be covered in writing about the issue of liberty and the Constitution.

HOW CAN THE CONSTITUTION SECURE THE BLESSINGS OF LIBERTY?

I. What is liberty?

A. Liberty and the ideas of the Enlightenment
   1. Voltaire's and Rousseau's notions of liberty
   2. Liberty during the French Revolution

B. Liberty as it evolved in America
   1. Patrick Henry: "Give me liberty or give me death!"
   2. Liberty Bell
   3. Statue of Liberty
   4. "Liberty and justice for all" from the *Pledge of Allegiance*
   5. "Do your own thing!" from the 1960s

II. The Constitution's concerns with liberty

A. Preamble
   1. "Establish justice"
   2. "Secure the blessings of liberty to ourselves and our posterity"

B. Articles
   1. Separation of powers
   2. Trial by jury of peers

C. Bill of Rights
   1. Guaranteed basic freedoms
      a. Religion
      b. Speech; the press
      c. Peaceable assembly
      d. Right to bear arms
      e. No unreasonable search and seizure
      f. No double jeopardy
      g. No self-incrimination
      h. No cruel and unusual punishment

D. Amendments
   1. Demonstrated a changing concept of liberty
      a. Thirteenth Amendment prohibited slavery
      b. Nineteenth Amendment guaranteed women's suffrage
   2. Allowed flexibility to adapt to an evolving concept of liberty

III. Liberty is not an absolute concept

A. Contradictions among the colonists
   1. Fought for freedom against the British
   2. Had little concern for freedom of African-Americans, Native Americans, and women

B. Contradictions between different interest groups
   1. Right to smoke versus right to clean air
   2. Right to bear arms versus right to security from guns
   3. Right to drive versus right to drive recklessly

IV. Liberty versus regulation

A. Can liberty be defined in a way that pleases everyone?

B. How should conflicting opinions of liberty be reconciled?

BRIEF SUMMARY OF THE PARTS OF THE CONSTITUTION

Preamble

Sets forth the broad goals of the Constitution, which include providing justice, freedom, and security for the people of America.

Article One: Legislative Branch

Section 1:

- sets up bicameral (two-house) legislature

House of Representatives

Section 2:

- states decide who can vote for representatives
- sets requirements for representatives: 25 years old, citizen for seven years, resident of state
- number of representatives are selected according to population of the state
- states fill vacancies
- power of impeachment ("accusation")
- representatives choose their speaker and officers

Senate

Section 3:

- senators are selected by state legislators (this was changed in 1913 by the Seventeenth Amendment)
- staggers six-year terms; one-third have elections every two years
- sets requirements for representatives: 30 years old, citizen for nine years, resident of state
- vice-president casts tie-breaking votes when necessary
- the Senate chooses its officers
- powers of impeachment
- impeachment removes officials from office and disqualifies them for future office, but it does not protect them from criminal prosecution by courts of law

Congress Operating Procedures

Section 4:

- elections and meetings are decided by state districts
- Congress assembles on the first Monday of each December (this was changed to January 3rd by the Twentieth Amendment)

Section 5:

- each house judges elections and member qualification
- each house determines its own rules of order
- each house keeps records of its proceedings
- houses cannot go on strike

Section 6:

- payment and privileges of legislatures

How a Bill Becomes a Law

Section 7:

- the House of Representatives originates money bills
- executive veto power
- the Congress cannot bypass the president by disguising the law as a resolution

Congressional Powers

Section 8:

- taxation
- borrowing
- foreign commerce
- naturalization
- bankruptcy
- currency
- standards
- counterfeiting
- post offices, post roads
- patents, copyrights
- federal courts
- maritime crimes
- declaration of war
- armed forces
- militia
- District of Columbia
- law making

Powers Forbidden to Congress

Section 9:

- cannot prohibit slavery before 1808
- cannot suspend "habeas corpus" (an arrested person must be brought to court to determine whether the arrest was legal)
- no "ex post facto" law (retroactively making a legal act a crime)
- no taxes unless in proportion with the census; no taxes on interstate exports
- no economic preference to any state
- money taken from the treasury must be accounted for
- no title of nobility

Powers Forbidden to States

Section 10:

- no treaties, coining money, titles, etc.
- no import or export duties
- no foreign relations or war powers

Article Two: Executive Branch

President and Vice-President

Section 1:

- four-year terms
- electors are selected by the state legislatures
- electors meet to vote (this was superseded by the Twelfth Amendment)
- the Congress picks the time to choose electors (voting day is always the first Tuesday after the first Monday in November)
- must be a natural born citizen, 35 years old, resident of the U.S. for 14 years
- succession if the president dies, resigns, or is otherwise unable to continue (see Twenty-fifth Amendment and 1948 law)
- salaries and expense allowances
- oath of office

Section 2:

- civilian in charge of the military
- only Congress can declare war
- basis for cabinet
- treaties
- ambassadors
- fill vacancies during Senate races

Section 3:

- State of the Union
- budget
- economic report
- special messages

Section 4:

- reasons for impeachment

Article Three: Judicial Branch

Federal Court's Jurisdiction

Section 1:

- one Supreme Court
- Congress creates inferior courts as necessary

Section 2:

- power in cases concerning law and equity
- cases affecting ambassadors, public ministers, and consuls have original jurisdiction
- admiralty and maritime
- controversies between two or more states (this was changed by the Twentieth Amendment)
- trial by jury guaranteed

Section 3:

- definition of treason
- treason only pertains to offender

Article Four: The States

Duties and Rights of the States

Section 1:

- prevents a person from crossing state lines to avoid court action

Citizens' Rights and Liabilities

Section 2:

- right in one state carry over to another (*e.g.*, marriage)
- a criminal who flees to a different state can be returned to the state where he perpetrated the crime
- a person obligated to service in one state (slavery) cannot escape it by going to another state (this was made obsolete by the Thirteenth Amendment)

New States

Section 3:

- new states admitted by Congress
- a new state cannot be formed within an existing state
- a new state cannot be formed by two states joining together
- Congress has the power to govern and make rules about U.S.-owned territory

Guarantees to States

Section 4:

- republican form of government
- protection from invasion
- protection from domestic violence when requested

Article Five: Amending the Constitution

- two-thirds vote by both houses
- two-thirds vote by state legislature to hold a convention
- ratification by three-fourths means approval

Article Six: Supreme Law

- laws and treaties are supreme (no higher authority)
- legislators must take oath
- no religious test required

Article Seven: Ratification

- ratification by nine states

Bill of Rights (First Ten Amendments)

1. Freedom of religion, press, speech, assembly, petition
2. Right to keep and bear arms
3. Cannot quarter soldiers in a person's house without consent
4. Freedom from unreasonable searches and seizures
5. Grand jury, no double jeopardy, no self-incrimination
6. Accused persons have rights to a speedy, impartial trial and an impartial jury
7. Trial by jury
8. No excessive fines or cruel and unusual punishment
9. Constitution does not preclude other rights
10. Powers not mentioned reserved for states and people

CHRONOLOGY

Amendments to the Constitution

1798 **Amendment 11** changes Article Three, Section 2: one state cannot be sued in another state.

1804 **Amendment 12** replaces Article Two, Section 1; adjusts the Constitution to national parties and gives each elector one vote instead of two.

1865 **Amendment 13** prohibits slavery.

1868 **Amendment 14** rejects southern doctrines of state rights versus federal.

1870 **Amendment 15** forbids the denial of suffrage because of race, color, or previous servitude.

1913 **Amendment 16** establishes a federal income tax.

1913 **Amendment 17** allows senators to be elected popularly instead of through the state legislature.

1919 **Amendment 18** imposes prohibition of liquor.

1920 **Amendment 19** gives women the right to vote.

1933 **Amendment 20** shortens period with "lame duck" president; provides for succession to president in certain situations.

1933 **Amendment 21** repeals prohibition.

1951 **Amendment 22** limits presidential terms to two.

1961 **Amendment 23** allows District of Columbia residents to vote for president and vice-president.

1964 **Amendment 24** bars poll tax.

1967 **Amendment 25** institutes presidential succession and disability.

1971 **Amendment 26** gives 18-year-olds the right to vote.

1992 **Amendment 27** limits the ability of congress to raise its own salary.

SHORT READING LIST

Robert A. Goldwin and William A. Schambra, eds., *How Democratic is the Constitution?* Presents a variety of opinions on the Constitution's strengths and weaknesses with respect to providing a true democracy.

Alan P. Grimes, *Democracy and the Amendments to the Constitution.* Provides in-depth background on the formulation and historical significance of constitutional amendments.

Alfred Kelly, *The American Constitution.* Covers constitutional development since colonial days.

Leonard Levy, ed., *Essays on the Making of the Constitution.* Provides a wide variety of perspectives about the creation of the Constitution.

J.W. Peltason, *Understanding the Constitution.* Explains the Constitution section by section.

Edward S. Corwin, ed., *The Constitution and What It Means Today.* Breaks down the Constitution and examines it in detail.

Leonard W. Levy, Kenneth L. Karst, and Dennis J. Mahoney, eds., *Encyclopedia of the American Constitution*, 4 vols. Includes approximately 2,220 articles on the Constitution.

John Kukla, ed., *The Bill of Rights: A Lively Heritage.* Captures the passion behind the push for the Bill of Rights.

James L. Sundquist, *Constitutional Reform and Effective Government.* Looks at amendments to the Constitution and Supreme Court decisions.

Alexis de Tocqueville, *Democracy in America.* Famous text that gives a French statesman's view of the U.S. democratic system.

Chapter

The Legislative Branch

MAJOR THEMES AND QUESTIONS

Bicameral System

1. In what ways are senators more powerful than representatives?
2. How does size change the activities the Senate engages in, such as debate on the Senate floor, etc.?
3. Of the House and Senate, which has traditionally been more pluralistic?
4. Would a constituent be better off appealing to a senator or a representative concerning a problem in a local district?
5. Does the bicameral system favor small states?
6. What duties do the House and Senate share?
7. Why does the Constitution assign certain duties, such as ratifying treaties and confirming presidential appointments, to the Senate?
8. How did the Seventeenth Amendment change the way senators are elected?
9. How are congressional seats apportioned?
10. Why are House seats reapportioned every 10 years? What are the political consequences of this?
11. What are the powers of the Speaker of the House?
12. What is the president of the Senate and the president pro tempore?
13. For what reasons are joint sessions of both houses called?
14. What are some circumstances in which the two houses have become deadlocked?

Legislative Powers

1. What is the difference between expressed and implied powers?
2. What have been some historical interpretations and ramifications of Article One, Section 8, clause 1 of the Constitution, which states that the Congress has the power to "provide for the common defense and general welfare of the United States"?
3. Discuss how the powers to "lay and collect taxes, duties, imposts, and excises" (Article One, Section 8) are keys to the system of federalism.

ROAD MAP

- *Major Themes and Questions*
  - *Bicameral System*
  - *Legislative Powers*
  - *Organization of Congress*
  - *Making a Law*
- *Major Terms and Concepts*
- *Chronology*
- *Short Reading List*

4. What is the purpose of Congress issuing copyrights and patents?
5. What power does Congress have over federal courts?
6. Describe the historical struggle for power between the legislative and judicial branches of government in terms of "checks and balances."
7. Why is the legislative veto a controversial power?
8. In what ways has Congress's nonlegislative power of "advice and consent" worked as a check on presidential power?
9. Are Senate hearings for presidential appointments, such as those for Supreme Court Justice nominees Bork, Kennedy, and Thomas, merely "political," or are they a useful function of democracy?
10. Discuss "pork-barrel politics" as an abuse of Congressional power.
11. Is it reasonable for legislators to fight for federal contracts in order to benefit their home states or districts, or is this harmful to the country as a whole?
12. How is the Congress regulated for abuse of power? Discuss the abuse of power in terms of the Savings and Loan scandal of the 1980s or similar scandals.
13. What is the code of ethics created by both houses?
14. Discuss whether the franking privilege and other perquisites for members of Congress are necessary.
15. Is the Speaker of the House more powerful than the president?

Organization of Congress

1. When can the president call a special session of Congress?
2. What are some informal rules of Congress?
3. To what extent does reciprocity of political favors keep the mechanism of Congress functioning?
4. What are the functions of the whips and floor leaders?
5. What is the importance of seniority, and how does a legislator gain seniority?
6. Has the seniority system always put the most competent legislators in power? Explain.
7. Describe some of the famous congressional compromises.
8. What measures have been taken to limit the cost of congressional staffs?
9. Describe the functions and skills of a typical congressional staff.
10. What supports do the Library of Congress, General Accounting Office, Congressional Budget Office, and the Office of Technological Assessment give to the Congress?

Making a Law

1. What is the role of committees in making a law?
2. Why do legislators compete to be on certain committees?
3. Describe the steps taken for a bill to become a law.
4. What materials are submitted to committees and subcommittees?
5. How has the filibuster been used historically to stop controversial legislation?
6. Why is it necessary for the two chambers to work together to pass a bill?
7. Discuss the importance of the congressional calendar to the passage of bills.
8. How does the president check the Congress's power to make laws?

MAJOR TERMS AND CONCEPTS

Organization and Power

bicameral
minority leader
standing committee
conference committee
steering committees
steering and policy committee
power to regulate interstate commerce
forbidden powers
war powers
gerrymandering
reapportionment
Speaker of the House
seniority
elastic clause
"one man, one vote"
perquisites
Savings and Loan scandal
president pro tempore
legislative assistant
caseworkers
congressional oversight
cloture
minority whip
special committee
joint committee
subcommittee
committee on committees
power to recognize
power to tax
expressed powers
implied powers
pork barrel
session of Congress
franking privilege
term of Congress
"necessary and proper" clause
Abscam
constituency service
confirmation process
caucus
administrative assistant
press aide
logrolling

Making Laws

lobbying
Union Calendar
House Calendar
Consent Calendar
Calendar of Business
Private Calendar
Executive Calendar
open rule
closed rule
modified rule
appropriation bills
amendments
filibuster
line-item veto
table
discharge petition
suspension of rules
riders
unanimous consent agreements
House-Senate Conference Committee
override
floor debate

SAMPLE OUTLINE

In the system of checks and balances, there is constant competition for power between the three branches of government. The question of one branch's power overshadowing another's is a natural concern in such a system. Many analysts have pointed to the growing power of the Congress as a discernible trend. If such a trend indeed exists, it could be illustrated by tracing its chronological development and by showing a cause-and-effect relationship between historical events and powers acquired by the Congress. In this outline, the examination of Congress has been limited to approximately the last 60 years, since using the entire history of Congress would be too cumbersome and too general.

CONGRESS'S INCREASED POWER

I. The Constitution creates a flexible framework to allow change in the powers of Congress

- A. Elastic clause
  1. Necessary and proper clause
  2. *McCulloch v. Maryland*
- B. Amendments to the Constitution
  1. Sixteenth Amendment
  2. Seventeenth Amendment

II. The period between the FDR and Nixon presidencies was a low point in congressional power

- A. Secondary role in making national policy
  1. New Deal and World War II
     - a. FDR used the seriousness of the Great Depression to force his policies into action
     - b. World War II demanded strong executive action of the commander in chief
  2. Great Society
     - a. Ideological successor of the New Deal
     - b. Johnson was a skillful legislator able to use Congress for his own purposes
  3. Most post-1945 foreign policy initiatives came from the executive branch
     - a. UN
     - b. NATO
     - c. Korean War
     - d. Vietnam War

III. Problems with Vietnam policy resulted in a decrease of presidential dominance over Congress

- A. War Powers Resolution of 1973
  1. Limited presidential power to wage war
  2. Congressional approval needed to commit troops for more than 60 days
- B. Congressional Budget and Impoundment Control Act of 1974
  1. Congress has more control over fiscal matters
  2. Power to review the president's entire budget

C. Congress has challenged administrations since Gerald Ford
   1. American troops in Lebanon
   2. Size of defense budget
   3. Ratification of SALT II
   4. Dealings with Iran
   5. Money for Contras in Nicaragua

IV. Many reforms have been initiated by Congress

A. Clean Air Act of 1970
B. Federal Campaign Reform Act of 1974
C. Strip Mining Act of 1977
D. Omnibus Anti-Drug Act of 1986

V. Some perceive increased congressional power as dangerous

A. Ronald Reagan resented Congress for interfering with his foreign policy
   1. Lack of support for Contras
   2. Curbs on military spending
B. George Bush's presidency was marred by its perception as a deadlocked government
   1. "Forced" by Congress to increase taxes
   2. Unable to pass the budget he promised the electorate

VI. Others perceive Congress as regaining powers that they deserve

A. Congress has the necessary expertise
   1. Creation of the Congressional Budget Office and Office of Technological Assessment
   2. More professional staffers
B. Congress represents the people more directly
   1. Congress has become more democratic
      a. Open procedures
      b. Less strict seniority system
      c. Committee sessions open to the public
   2. Congressional members hear from people in their local districts
   3. House members are elected more frequently
   4. Congressional members historically come from more diverse backgrounds than do presidents

CHRONOLOGY

Supreme Court Cases Affecting Congressional Power

1819 *McCulloch v. Maryland* reinforced the doctrine of implied powers of the Congress. The case centered around whether the state of Maryland could tax notes issued by the Bank of the United States. Justice Marshall, speaking for the Court, stated that in accordance with Article One, Section 8 of the Constitution, the Congress is not limited solely to the enactment of laws, but can also do what is necessary to fulfill all the powers granted to it. "Let the end be legitimate, let it be within the scope of the Constitution, and all means which are appropriate, which are plainly adapted to that end, which are not prohibited, but consistent with the letter and spirit of the Constitution, are constitutional." Since the Maryland tax would have impeded powers of the federal government, which has supremacy in such cases, it was declared unconstitutional.

1824 *Gibbons v. Ogden* reaffirmed the Congress's power to regulate interstate commerce, broadening its definition to include any transaction that was even partially conducted in more than one state.

1870 *Collector v. Day* made state instrumentalities exempt from federal tax. The Supreme Court used the same reasoning as in the *McCulloch v. Maryland* ruling, except that this time, it was for the protection of states' rights.

1881 *Kilbourn v. Thompson* limited the investigating powers of Congress to the areas in which it legislates.

1894–95 *Pollock v. Farmers' Loan and Trust Co.* declared Congress's act of 1894, which imposed an income tax without apportionment, to be unconstitutional since a tax on income is no different than a tax on land; therefore, it is a direct tax. In 1895, the same principle was expanded to include income from stocks and bonds.

1900 *Knowlton v. Moore* allowed Congress to tax inheritances over $10,000 since such a tax is not considered a direct tax.

1900 *Stearns v. Minnesota* upheld that the Congress's restrictions on the taxation of public lands, which were imposed when Minnesota entered into the Union, were lawful since they did not impair the rights of the states.

1905 *South Carolina v. United States* allowed the Congress to impose federal excise taxes on liquor stores in South Carolina since the stores were not instrumentalities of the government.

1911 *Coyle v. Smith* denied the power of Congress to prevent Oklahoma from changing the location of its state capital since that was considered a matter of state policy.

1922 *Bailey v. Drexel Furniture Co.* declared an act of Congress that had imposed a 10 percent tax on the net profits of any establishment that knowingly hired minors unconstitutionally on the grounds that the hiring of minors is subject to police regulation, and is not a matter of taxation.

1923 *Massachusetts v. Mellon* became another victory of federal power over states' power by denying an application of Massachusetts that was intended to prevent the secretary of the treasury from disbursing funds for maternal welfare.

1939 *Coleman v. Miller* gave Congress, not the courts, power to rule on the time permitted and validity of state ratification. The case evolved from the Kansas legislatures' slowness in ratifying a proposed child labor amendment that the Congress had submitted.

1946 *Colgrove v. Green* confirmed that the authority to redistrict a state belongs not to the courts but to Congress under Article One, Section 4 of the Constitution.

1964 *Wesberry v. Sanders* overruled *Colegrove v. Green* on the grounds that representatives in Congress must nearly as possible represent an equal number of people.

1969 *Powell v. McCormack* maintained that a two-thirds vote and not a majority vote was needed to change the constitutional qualifications of age, residence, and citizenship. The idea behind this was that the inhabitants of a congressional district are entitled to representation of their choosing. The case centered around a movement to deny Adam Clayton Powell his seat because of allegations of misuse of funds.

1972 *Gravel v. United States* prevented a congressional member's right of immunity from being "questioned in any other place" than a committee or legislative chamber to aides.

SHORT READING LIST

Roger H. Davidson and Walter J. Oleszek, *Congress and its Members*. Gives a general overview discussing members of Congress and how Congress works.

David J. Volger, *The Politics of Congress*, 4th ed. Gives a complete overview of the mechanization of Congress.

W. Wilson, *Congressional Government*. Written in 1885, this work gives a classic interpretation of the Congress.

J.W. Baker, ed., *Member of the House: Letters of a Congressman.* An informal look at Congress through the eyes of the late Congressman Clem Miller.

C.L. Clap, *The Congressman: His Work as He Sees It.* A number of congressmen provide their personal views.

W.S. White, *Citadel: The Story of the United States Senate*. Provides a very readable history of the Senate. Gives a good idea of the "unwritten rules."

Steven S. Smith and Christopher J. Deering, *Committees in Congress.* Gives a detailed analysis of the workings of congressional committees.

Gerald C. Wright, Jr., Leroy N. Riesbach, and Lawrence C. Dodds, eds., *Congress and Policy Change.* Gives a good sense of the power of Congress to influence public policy. It describes Congress during its powerful post-Vietnam era.

Stephen K. Bailey, *Congress Makes a Law.* Through the description of one law passed in 1946, an in-depth view of the passage of a legislation through Congress is presented.

Larry Dodd and Bruce Oppenheimer, eds., *Congress Reconsidered*, 3rd ed. Published most recently in 1985, this collection of studies gives an up-to-date account of the Congress.

Richard F. Fenno, Jr., *Bicameral Perspective.* Compares the two houses of Congress in terms of function and relative power.

Morris P. Fiorina, *Congress: Keystone of the Washington Establishment*. Examines the trend toward more and more members of Congress being reelected and how this affects the way Congress performs its duties.

Mark Green, et al., *Who Runs Congress?* Provides a critical examination of the underlying power structure controlling Congress. Since this is from the Ralph Nader group, it gives analysis from the point of view of the average constituent (consumer).

Michael J. Malbin, *Unelected Representatives*. Examines the considerable power and expertise of congressional staffs.

Howard McCurdy, *An Insider's Guide to the Capitol*. Provides an intimate view of Congress.

Eric Redman, *The Dance of Legislation*. A sometimes amusing account of the twists and turns a bill takes on its way to being passed or defeated.

Chapter

The Executive Branch

MAJOR THEMES AND QUESTIONS

Presidential Powers

1. To what extent have presidents been loyal to their parties when performing their jobs?
2. How has the media changed the president's relationship to the U.S. public?
3. What are the strengths and weaknesses of having the leader of the U.S. perform the ceremonial duties of the chief of state as well as the tasks of a head of government?
4. What concern caused the founders of the Constitution to allow only natural-born, not naturalized, citizens to be president?
5. Compare Theodore Roosevelt's "stewardship theory" interpretation of the office of president with Taft's "constitutional theory."
6. What was Supreme Court Justice Robert H. Jackson's view of the presidency in the "steel seizure case"?
7. Article Two, Section 2 of the Constitution gives the president power to make appointments for what offices?
8. How have executive agreements increased the president's diplomatic powers?
9. Explain the importance of the Supreme Court cases *Myers v. United States* (1926) and *Humphrey's Executor v. United States* (1935) in terms of the president's power to remove non-civil-service appointees.
10. Discuss President Ford's pardon of Richard Nixon in terms of the original intent of the Chief Executive's power to give pardons laid out in Article Two, Section 2 of the Constitution.
11. Compare Wilson's handling of the Versailles treaty with FDR's and Truman's handling of the United Nations Treaty and North Atlantic Treaty Organization.
12. Explain Richard Neustadt's theory that a president's main power is to persuade and not simply to act.
13. What has been the historical significance of giving the president special powers as commander in chief (Article Two, Section 2)?
14. What has traditionally been the role of presidents as leaders of their parties?
15. How can a president use impoundments to control spending?
16. Discuss *United States v. Nixon* in terms of executive privilege.

ROAD MAP

17. What is an impeachable offense? Use the cases of Presidents Andrew Johnson and Richard Nixon to discuss this question.
18. Explain the two-presidency thesis.
19. What is a line-item veto, and why have presidents like George Bush persistently requested it?

Growth and Change in the Job of President

1. What are the qualifications of the president set up by the Constitution?
2. Describe the changes in the presidency resulting from FDR's administration and the Twenty-second Amendment.
3. Compare George Washington's explicit and implicit precedents set for the job of president to the actual powers and functions of a modern president.
4. Why do some people support a single six-year term for the president?
5. How does the Twenty-fifth Amendment deal with the question of presidential succession and disability?
6. What have recent presidents done to make the office of the vice-president more practically functional?
7. Three of the first six presidents never vetoed legislation. How does that contrast to modern presidents?
8. Why were early Presidents Thomas Jefferson and James Monroe mainly concerned with foreign affairs?
9. What did Andrew Jackson and Abraham Lincoln do to broaden the powers of the presidency?
10. How did Vietnam and Watergate weaken the presidency?
11. Discuss the pros and cons of the media's influence on the modern presidency.
12. What explains the growth of the White House bureaucracy?
13. How have contemporary presidents used appeals to the public to promote their positions?

Agencies and Organization of the Executive Office

1. Compare Eisenhower's, Ford's, and Reagan's leadership styles to Kennedy's and Carter's.
2. To what extent has the growth of the presidential bureaucracy been necessitated by forces outside the president, and to what extent has it been a result of the wants of modern presidents?
3. How important has political loyalty been to the selection of White House staffs?
4. What presidential appointees do not need Senate confirmation?
5. What is the function and history of the National Security Council?
6. What are the political and policy functions of the White House staff?
7. Why did the Congress establish the Executive Office in 1939?
8. What are the functions of the cabinet members?
9. Was the Iran-Contra affair an example of an Executive Office, which does not have to answer directly to the Congress or the people, out of control?
10. What can the Department of the Treasury do to influence the economy?

11. Why do some consider the federal bureaucracy to be the fourth branch of the government?
12. To what extent is the bureaucracy of the executive branch a spoils system?
13. What are the "kitchen cabinet" and "inner cabinet"?

MAJOR TERMS AND CONCEPTS

Constitutional Presidency

impeachment
executive agreements
armed forces
pardon
chief executive
natural-born citizen
vice president
constitutional monarchy
full pardon
dismissal
presidential succession
head of state
civilian supremacy of the chief of state
reprieve
executive order
Twenty-second Amendment
electoral college
diplomatic recognition
commander in chief
treaty

Executive Branch Cabinet and Advisers

cabinet
inner cabinet
outer cabinet
White House staff
secretary of state
secretary of the treasury
secretary of agriculture
secretary of commerce
secretary of health and human services
secretary of transportation
secretary of education
White House chief of staff
national security adviser
U.S. trade representative
United Nations ambassador
administrator, Environmental Protection Agency
secretary of defense
secretary of veterans' affairs
secretary of the interior
secretary of labor
secretary of housing and urban development
secretary of energy
attorney general
director, Office of Management and Budget
drug czar
chairman, Council of Economic Advisers
director, Central Intelligence Agency

Presidential Powers

heroic president
tethered president
stewardship theory
steel seizure case
removal of power
the administration
Iran-Contra affair
commuted sentence
imperial president
two-presidency thesis
constitutional theory
power of appointment
power to pardon
Watergate affair
"coattail effect"
summit conference

SAMPLE OUTLINE

In the previous chapter, the sample outline dealt with the question of Congress's increasing power. To show that there are a variety of ways to deal with essays concerning governmental and political issues, this essay (like the previous one) will examine the power of one branch of the federal government: the executive branch. Instead of using a chronological progression, as the previous essay did, this essay will defend the thesis that the president has very few direct powers by using historical examples and a selective description of the various roadblocks hindering the president's direct power. This thesis has been most persuasively argued by author Richard Neustadt (see this unit's *Short Reading List*).

PRESIDENTIAL POWER: THE POWER TO PERSUADE

I. Persuasiveness is an important political tool

- A. Presidents get elected through their ability to persuade an electorate
  - 1. Many famous speeches have been turning points in candidacies and presidencies
    - a. Wilson's selling of the Versailles treaty—unsuccessful
    - b. Nixon's "Checkers" speech—successful
  - 2. Modern media give presidents more direct contact with people
    - a. Abundance of news programs
    - b. Presidents and candidates hire media specialists

II. There are many impediments and restrictions to presidential power

- A. Separation of powers restricts the president's authority
  - 1. Cannot order compliance of Congress or judiciary
  - 2. Congressmen have local constituencies and different needs than the president
  - 3. Federalism keeps presidents from controlling state officials
- B. The federal bureaucracy does not always cooperate
  - 1. Bureaucrats see many presidents come and go
    - a. More loyal to the job than to the president
    - b. Resent presidents for cutting or changing programs
  - 2. A president can only try to win cooperation

III. Many historical cases show limits to presidential power

- A. Cuban Missile Crisis should have been an example of a president at the height of his power
  - 1. Kennedy was limited by the military
    - a. Willingness to mobilize
    - b. Ability to mobilize
  - 2. Cabinet members resisted his original plan
    - a. Some felt a quick military strike was best
    - b. Consensus was important in order to avoid press leaks, etc.
- B. Bush made the campaign promise "Read my lips, no new taxes"
  - 1. Clearly pledged no tax hike
  - 2. Presented image of someone with authority to control taxation
  - 3. No consensus was reached among legislators that tax increases were avoidable
  - 4. Taxes were raised
  - 5. Bush blamed Congress for not following his wishes

IV. Persuasive presidents have been successful presidents

A. Lyndon B. Johnson successfully passed his legislation

1. Senate leadership taught him how to build coalitions
2. Passed "Great Society" legislation in spite of Republican opposition

B. Jimmy Carter, an "outsider," had a poor legislative record

1. As an outsider, he tried to avoid bargaining
2. Without congressional support, he was weakened

CHRONOLOGY

Supreme Court Cases Directly Affecting Executive Power

1827 *Martin v. Mott* held that under Article One, Section 8 of the Constitution, the president has the sole authority to judge whether calling forth a militia is necessary, and that all must follow his decision.

1829 *Foster v. Nelson* strengthened the president's power in foreign affairs by declaring his and Congress's decisions concerning the rights of the United States in foreign affairs to be binding and out of the jurisdiction of the courts. The case centered on a dispute between the U.S. and Spain over territory claimed by the U.S. as part of the Louisiana Purchase.

1838 *Kendall v. United States* prevented the president from forbidding a government officer—the postmaster general—to perform a duty imposed on him by the Congress.

1863 The Prize cases were four court decisions concerning southern vessels that were captured by the North after 1861. President Lincoln's action was sustained, stating that "if a war be made by invasion of a foreign nation, the president is not only authorized but bound to resist force, by force. He does not initiate the war, but is bound to accept the challenge without waiting for any special legislative authority. And whether the hostile party be a foreign invader, or States organized in rebellion, it is nonetheless a war...."

1867 *Mississippi v. Johnson* reinforced the president's power as an executive who is given flexible power so that he can use his discretion to enforce laws. Using this reasoning, Mississippi was not allowed to obtain an injunction to prevent one of the Reconstruction acts.

1893 *Fong Yue Ting v. United States* upheld the president's right to deport a native of China who came to the U.S. before the 1879 Chinese Exclusion Act that forbade Chinese immigration. This case reaffirmed that the president has sole discretion in matters of deportation.

1895 In re Debs upheld President Grover Cleveland's right to send in troops to deal with striking Pullman Company employees. The objection of the Governor of Illinois was not heeded since the Supreme Court upheld the government's right to limit monopolies and other combinations (as a trade union is considered) through its interstate commerce regulatory power.

1920 *Missouri v. Holland* reasserted the federal government's wildlife conservation rights, which had been previously usurped by lower courts. It allowed the executive branch to enforce a treaty with Great Britain for the protection of migratory birds.

1925 Ex parte Grossman used the argument of precedents in England and the U.S. to support the president's right to pardon a criminal convicted by a federal court.

1935 *Humphrey's Executor (Rathbun) v. United States* modified *Myers v. United States* by stating that the Federal Trade Commission, which was created by the Congress, was constitutional and that the president did not have control of the officers of the commission.

1936 *United States v. Curtiss-Wright Export Corporation* upheld the president's right to impose an embargo without Congress's approval. It states that "the President is the sole organ of the federal government in the field of international relations—a power that does not require as a basis for its exercise an act of Congress, but which of course, like every other governmental power, must be exercised in subordination to the applicable provisions of the Constitution."

1937 *United States v. Belmont* sustained FDR's right to start diplomatic relations with the Soviet Union. This once again asserted the federal government's authority over the states by going against a New York State law.

1958 *Kent v. Dulles* held that when the secretary of state issues passports, he must hold to restrictions established by usage and authorized by Congress.

1958 *Wiener v. United States* stated that the president cannot remove members of the War Claims Commission because their functions are intrinsically judicial.

1964 *Aptheker v. Secretary of State* declared unconstitutional the denial of passports to citizens who were required to register with the attorney general under the Internal Security Act of 1950.

SHORT READING LIST

W. Binkley, *The Man in the White House*. Explains the growth and the many facets of the office of president.

E. S. Corwin, *The President: Office and Powers*. Gives a comprehensive overview of the historical and constitutional development of the presidency.

R. Neustadt, *Presidential Power*. This is a highly influential and interpretive work that makes a case for the limits of presidential power.

H. J. Laski, *The American Presidency.* Provides a British perspective of the presidency.

H. L. Laurin, *Presidential Transitions*. Discusses the changes and problems that occur in the transition from the election to the inauguration.

L. D. White, *The Federalists*, *The Jeffersonians*, *The Jacksonians*, and *The Republican Era*. These works cover the early years of the Republic, with an emphasis on the organization of the executive branch.

R. J. Donovan, *The Inside Story*, and E. J. Hughes, *The Ordeal of Power: A Political Memoir of the Eisenhower Years*. These works detail cabinet meetings and provide an inside view of politics during Eisenhower's presidency.

Michael R. Beschloss, *The Crisis Years*. Uses recently released documents to give new, detailed insight into decision-making processes during Kennedy's tenure.

A. M. Schlesinger, Jr., *A Thousand Days*. Provides an intimate portrait of Kennedy, the man, as well as Kennedy, the president.

R. F. Fenno, Jr., *The President's Cabinet*. Analyzes cabinets of Presidents from Wilson to Eisenhower.

George C. Edwards III and Stephen J. Wayne, *Presidential Leadership*. Provides a current assessment of the state of the presidency.

Gary King and Lyn Ragsdale, *The Elusive Executive: Discovering Statistical Patterns in the Presidency*. Uses statistics to interpret actions and results of the executive branch.

John E. Mueller, *War, Presidents and Public Opinion*. Uses public opinion polls to draw general conclusions about the effects of wars and crises on a president's popularity.

Beryl A. Radin and Willis D. Hawley, *The Politics of Federal Reorganization: Creating the U.S. Department of Education*. Gives insight into the federal bureaucracy by describing its recent major changes.

Thomas E. Cronin, ed., *Rethinking the Presidency*. Assesses the changing power of the president through various articles.

Chapter

The Judicial Branch

MAJOR THEMES AND QUESTIONS

Organization of the Judicial Branch

1. How are the various types of courts different?
2. Explain the hierarchy between the U.S. Supreme Court, U.S. court of appeals, and U.S. district courts.
3. In what situations do cases in state courts get passed on to the U.S. Supreme Court?
4. What problem did the Eleventh Amendment address?
5. What provisions in the Constitution attempt to keep the selection and actions of Supreme Court justices nonpolitical?
6. Why have many charged that the nominating process for recent Supreme Court appointees (*e.g.*, Judges Bork and Thomas) has become too political?
7. Which courts have original jurisdiction in most cases?
8. When and why were courts of appeal established?
9. What is the difference between statutory law, administrative law, and constitutional law?
10. How does the Supreme Court decide which cases to consider?
11. In what situation does the Supreme Court use per curiam opinion?
12. Discuss the importance of majority opinion as the official voice of the Supreme Court.
13. What are the concurring and dissenting opinions of the Supreme Court?
14. What is Charles Johnson and Bradley Canon's three-step model for implementation of judicial policy making?
15. Describe the five major stages of how cases are decided by the Supreme Court: petition for review, briefs on merits, oral argument, conference and decision, and assignment and writing of opinions.

Role of the Supreme Court

1. Compare Justice Hugo L. Black, a judicial activist, with Justice Felix Frankfurter, a judicial restraintist.
2. Why was *Marbury v. Madison* a landmark case in terms of the legal and political role of the Supreme Court?

ROAD MAP

3. Article Two, Section 2 of the Constitution gives the president power to appoint federal judges "by and with the advice and consent of the Senate." Why has this been a cause for disagreement?
4. Discuss the Court's discovery of legislative intent in terms of the relationship between the judicial and legislative branches.
5. Discuss how the language in the Constitution allows for competing constitutional values among justices.
6. Discuss the meaning of judicial review.
7. Explain how the decisions of a Supreme Court justice can be affected by his/her political ideas, perception of social roles, and by whether he/she is result- or process-oriented.
8. Discuss the quotes "courts are the mere instruments of the law, and can will nothing" (Chief Justice John Marshall) and "judicial decisions are not babies brought by constitutional storks" (Max Lerner).

Landmark Cases

1. What was Chief Justice John Marshall's judicial logic for declaring the Judiciary Act of 1789 unconstitutional?
2. Why is it that *Marbury v. Madison*, a case over a relatively trivial matter, is considered to have established the cornerstone of judicial review?
3. How did the *McCulloch v. Maryland* decision interpret the implied powers clause of the Constitution?
4. How did *Gibbons v. Ogden* settle once and for all the extent of federal power in relation to state power?
5. To what extent did *Dred Scott v. Sandford* work as a catalyst for the Civil War?
6. What effect did *Munn v. Illinois and Northern Securities Company et al. v. United States* have in terms of controlling the actions of big business?
7. What major change in race relations in the U.S. was reflected in the *Brown v. Board of Education of Topeka*?
8. Describe the problems encountered with the enforcement of *Brown v. Board of Education of Topeka*.
9. Discuss *Miranda v. Arizona* in terms of changes in the rights of the accused.
10. Why is *Roe v. Wade* such a controversial decision?

MAJOR TERMS AND CONCEPTS

Chief Justices (chronological order)

Jay
Rutledge
Marshall
Taney
Chase
Waite
Fuller
Taft
White
Hughes
Stone
Vinson
Warren
Burger
Rehnquist

Legal Terms

appellate jurisdiction
concurrent jurisdiction
original jurisdiction
diversity jurisdiction
exclusive jurisdiction
citizen's arrest
common law
contempt of court
directed verdict
equity
injunction
arraignment
misdemeanor
bill of indictment
petit jury
precedents
probate
subpoena
administrative law
summation
writ of certiorari
writ of mandamus
writ of habeas corpus
judicial activism
judicial review
restraint of trade
tort case
test case
probate case
charge
civil procedure
criminal procedure
arrest warrant
docket
bail
capital punishment
mistrial
perjury
plea
preliminary hearing
search warrant
statutory law
constitutional law
transcript
due process clause
judicial restraint
public welfare
selective incorporation
criminal case
civil case
domestic relations case
"separate but equal"
adversary proceeding
strict construction
implied powers
Jim Crow laws
exclusionary rule
senatorial courtesy
in forma pauperis
conference
amicus curiae
majority opinion
dissenting opinion

stare decisis
plea bargaining
loose construction
felony
civil liberties
reverse discrimination
certiorari
rule of four
per curiam opinion
concurring opinion
minority opinion

Types of Courts

Supreme Court
U.S. district courts
general trial court
municipal court
state appeals court
territorial courts
appellate court
court of military appeals
federal circuit court of appeals
immigration court
U.S. courts of appeals
claims court
juvenile court
small claims court
state supreme court
domestic relations court
tax courts
customs court
traffic court
country court

Legal Participants

judge
grand jury
recorder
prosecuting attorney
plaintiff
litigants
court stenographer
jury
foreman
public defender
defense attorney
defendant
bailiff
court officer

SAMPLE OUTLINE

THE STRUCTURE OF THE JUDICIAL BRANCH OF THE FEDERAL GOVERNMENT

I. Its purpose

A. To interpret the constitutionality of laws passed by Congress

B. To try cases where federal laws are involved

II. Kinds of courts

A. U.S. Supreme Court

1. Established by Article Three of the Constitution
2. Justices appointed for life by the president and approved by the Senate
3. Eight associate justices and one chief justice
4. Quorum is six members
5. Decisions made by majority vote
6. Hears appeals from federal courts if constitutionality is involved
7. Hears first-time cases involving states, federal government, president, Congress, ambassadors, or ministers

8. Hears appeals from state courts if federal constitutionality is involved
9. Reviews about 2,500 cases per year

B. U.S. courts of appeals (circuit courts)
   1. Established in 1891 by Congress
   2. Divided into 12 circuits or regions
   3. Justices appointed for life by president and approved by Senate
   4. Have from 5 to 27 justices and at least two per case
   5. Only appeals cases from district courts
   6. Review about 18,000 cases per year

C. U.S. district courts
   1. Established in 1789 during Washington's presidency
   2. Currently 91 courts divided among 50 states
   3. Have one judge and three judge cases
   4. Have original jurisdiction for cases involving federal laws and orders, fraud, tax evasion, suits between two states, etc.
   5. Hear 90 percent of all federal cases

D. U.S. special courts
   1. Court of international trade
   2. U.S. claims court
   3. U.S. tax court and tariff court
   4. Court of military appeals
   5. Federal circuit court of appeals
   6. Court of appeals for District of Columbia

E. State supreme courts
   1. Established according to state laws
   2. Final interpreter of state law
   3. Final court of appeal for lower court decisions
   4. Decisions final except when the case falls under concurrent jurisdiction of the U.S. Supreme Court

F. State appeals court
   1. Established in some states
   2. Like U.S. appeals courts, they lighten the state supreme court's burden

G. General trial courts
   1. Established as the first level of state courts
   2. Have both original and appellate jurisdiction

H. Local courts
   1. Municipal courts (for larger communities)
   2. Justice's courts (for minor cases in villages and small towns)
   3. Police courts (for minor cases in cities)

SAMPLE OUTLINE

Instead of making an argument for a particular point of view, as the previous outlines have done, this outline will try to accurately explain what most agree to be the most important decision made by the Supreme Court: *Marbury v. Madison*. To write a good essay on such a topic, one needs to divide the topic into three parts: the background events that caused the case, the arguments and decisions rendered in the case, and the significance of the case. This outline addresses these three parts in that order for purposes of logic and clarity.

MARBURY v. MADISION ESTABLISHES JUDICIAL REVIEW

I. John Adams, Federalist, lost election of 1800

- A. Old inauguration schedule: in office until March 3, 1801
  1. On his last day, made as many appointments as possible
  2. Rewarded Federalists with federal judgeships
- B. John Marshall made a minor procedural mistake
  1. Last posts were District of Columbia justices
  2. William Marbury was appointed
  3. Secretary of State John Marshall forgot to affix the Great Seal of the United States
- C. Jefferson, the new president, did not cooperate
  1. Was annoyed by the number of Federalist judges appointed
  2. Did not deliver the new commissions

II. Many important implications grew from the case

- A. Marbury asked Supreme Court to take original jurisdiction
  1. Judiciary Act of 1789
  2. Section 13
     - a. Writs of mandamus
     - b. Office under U.S. authority
- B. Marshall knew Madison would ignore writ
  1. Jefferson would likely back up secretary of state
  2. Jefferson had popular support
  3. Court would be unable to enforce its opinion
- C. Marshall used judicial logic to reason through the case
  1. There were two types of Supreme Court original jurisdiction
     - a. Cases involving foreign diplomats
     - b. Cases involving states
  2. Judiciary Act amended the Constitution
- D. Marbury's case was thrown out
  1. Congress could not change Constitution through an act
  2. Declared Judiciary Act of 1789 unconstitutional
  3. Marbury would have to pursue case in lower court

III. Marshall led Court to claim new power

A. Marbury did not receive his commission
B. Declaring an act unconstitutional set a precedent
C. Judicial review was neither given nor denied by the Constitution
D. Doctrine of judicial review emerged
   1. Oversees all acts of president or Congress
   2. Courts check constitutionality
E. Courts were made a co-equal in government

CHRONOLOGY

Important Supreme Court Cases

1803 *Marbury v. Madison* established the precedent for judicial review and declared an act of Congress unconstitutional for the first time.

1819 *McCulloch v. Maryland* resolved the issue of legislative responsibilities of Congress and gave a liberal interpretation of the implied powers clause of the Constitution.

1824 *Gibbons v. Ogden* established a federal regulation of interstate commerce, and broadened the definition of commerce while limiting state interference.

1857 *Dred Scott v. Sandford* recognized the legitimacy of slavery. Slavery could legally exist in any state.

1876 *Munn v. Illinois* asserted that states could regulate privately owned businesses for public interest. This case is a good example of judicial restraint.

1954 *Brown v. Board of Education of Topeka* reversed the "Separate but equal" precedent and showed the evolution of the Supreme Court on the issue of race.

1966 *Miranda v. Arizona* protected the rights of individuals accused of crimes. It is controversial because some say the rights of crime victims are diminished since it is now more difficult to get a criminal confession.

SHORT READING LIST

E. V. Rostow, *The Sovereign Prerogative: The Supreme Court and the Quest for Law*. A liberal evaluation of Supreme Court policy into the 1960s.

C. Warren, *The Supreme Court in United States History*, two vols. A standard history that gives a relatively sympathetic view of judicial review.

S. F. Konefsky, *The Legacy of Holmes and Brandeis*. Takes two well-known judges and gives an in-depth study of their constitutional philosophies.

Robert G. McClosky, *The American Supreme Court*. This is a survey of various landmark Supreme Court cases.

Henry J. Abraham, *Justices and Presidents*, 2nd ed. Gives insight into the politics behind appointments to the Supreme Court.

Walter F. Murphy, *Elements of Judicial Strategy*. Discusses the internal bargaining and other elements of the process that the Supreme Court goes through in order to reach a decision.

David M. O'Brien, *Storm Center: The Supreme Court in American Politics*. Examines the Supreme Court in the context of the larger political arena.

Lawrence Baum, *The Supreme Court*, 2nd ed. This short text covers both the structure and power of the Court.

Alexander M. Bickle, *The Least Dangerous Branch*. Presents an argument against strong judicial review.

Mark W. Cannon and David M. O'Brien, *Views From the Bench*. Gives a taste of judicial reasoning and a survey of famous issues and cases through the speeches and writings of Supreme Court justices.

Archibald Cox, *The Role of the Supreme Court in American Government*. Examines the Supreme Court in terms of its relationship to the other branches of government.

Jerome Frank, *Courts on Trial: Myth and Reality in American Justice*. Tries to eliminate inaccurate preconceptions about the judicial system in the U.S.

Leon Friedman and Fred Israel, eds., *The Justices of the United States Supreme Court 1789–1965: Their Lives and Major Opinions*. Gives interesting, readable biographies of Supreme Court justices.

Herbert Jacob, *Justice in America: Courts, Lawyers and the Judicial Process*, 4th ed. Describes various aspects of the court system.

Alpheus T. Mason, *The Supreme Court from Taft to Burger*. Gives a historical account up to the 1970s.

Chapter

Bureaucracy

MAJOR THEMES AND QUESTIONS

Growth and Change in the Bureaucracy

1. What accounts for the growth of a bureaucracy from 3,000 persons in 1800 to 95,000 in 1881 to one-half million in 1925 and over three million presently? Is this growth healthy?
2. Would the framers of the Constitution approve the size and scope of the federal bureaucracy in its present manifestation?
3. Why do some credit Andrew Jackson with creating a "spoils system"?
4. What relation was there between Garfield's assassination and the reform of government hiring practices?
5. Explain the Pendleton Act of 1883.
6. Explain the Hatch Act of 1939.
7. What have been some criticisms of the civil service system?
8. Explain the Civil Service Reform Act of 1978.
9. Why is it in a bureaucrat's interest to protect the size and scope of a program controlled by his/her agency, and how might this run contrary to the wishes of the president and Congress?
10. Is the bureaucracy the fourth branch of government?
11. How did President Carter influence federal bureaucracy with his Office of Personnel Management and Merit Systems Protection Board?

Interaction of Government Agencies and Branches

1. What influence does the president have over federal bureaucracies?
2. How did Reagan deal with uncooperative civil servants?
3. How can a president use the OMB (Office of Management and Budget) to influence the federal bureaucracy?
4. In what ways are the Congress's powers to control government stronger than the president's?
5. Explain Congress's disciplinary actions, such as overriding the FDA's ban on saccharin in the late 1970s and condemning HUD's spending on luxury condos in the late 1980s.
6. Why is area-specific expertise more important to the success of a bureaucrat than to that of a member of congress or the president?

ROAD MAP

- *Major Themes and Questions*
  - *Growth and Change in the Bureaucracy*
  - *Interaction of Government Agencies and Branches*
  - *Power and Rule of Government Agencies*
- *Major Terms and Concepts*
- *Sample Outline*
- *Chronology*
- *Short Reading List*

7. How does a bureaucrat balance the interests of the Congress with those of outside interest groups?
8. Explain the relationship between the executive independent regulatory commissions and government corporations.
9. How might congressional pork-barreling influence federal bureaucracy?
10. What is the "iron triangle"?
11. In what way is a "legislative veto" a means for the Congress to check the executive branch's control over most of the federal bureaucracy?

Power and Role of Government Agencies

1. Explain the process by which government agencies create legally binding regulations.
2. What might a business or citizen do about a federal agency's regulation when the regulation is considered unfair or unconstitutional?
3. Explain how bureaucrats translate policy ideas into action.
4. Discuss the success of the FDIC, in terms of the original purpose of its creation, with respect to the Savings and Loan scandal of the Reagan and Bush administrations.
5. Explain President Kennedy's quote, "It's good to have men like [Air Force General] Curt LeMay and [Navy Admiral] Arleigh Burke commanding troops once you decide to go in. But these men are not the only ones you should listen to when you decide whether to go in or not."

MAJOR TERMS AND CONCEPTS

Structure and Power of the Bureaucracy

affirmative action
"fourth branch"
regulatory authority
independent regulatory commissions
independent agencies
red tape
subsidies
commissioners
bureaucrats
executive agency
cabinet
rule-making
legislative veto
iron triangle
merit system
deregulation
spoils system
captured agencies
statutory law
veteran's preference
whistle-blower

Independent Agencies and Government Corporations

ACTION
Administration Conference of the United States
African Development Foundation
American Battle Monuments Commission
Appalachian Regional Commission
Arms Control and Disarmament Agency
Board of International Broadcasting
Central Intelligence Agency
Civil Aeronautics Board
Civil Service Commission

Commission of Fine Arts
Commission on Civil Rights
Commodity Futures Trading Commission
Community Services Administration
Consumer Products Safety Commission
Environmental Protection Agency
Employment Opportunity Commission
Farm Credit Administration
Federal Communications Commission
Federal Deposit Insurance Corporation
Federal Election Commission
Federal Emergency Management Agency
Federal Home Loan Bank Board
Federal Labor Relations Authority
Federal Maritime Commission
Federal Reserve System
Federal Retirement Thrift Investment Board
Federal Trade Commission
General Services Administration
Inter-American Foundation
International Commerce Agency
Interstate Commerce Commission
Merit Systems Protection Board
National Aeronautics and Space Administration
National Archives and Records Administration
National Capital Planning Commission
National Credit Union Administration
National Foundations on Arts and Humanities
National Labor Relations Board
National Mediation Board
National Rail Passenger Corporation
National Regulatory Commission
National Science Foundation
Occupational Safety and Health Review Commission
Office of Personnel Management
Overseas Private Investment Management
Panama Canal Commission
Peace Corps
Pennsylvania Ave. Development Corp.
Pension Benefit Guaranty Corporation
Postal Rate Commission
Railroad Retirement Board
Securities and Exchange Commission
Selective Service System
Small Business Commission
Tennessee Valley Authority
U.S. Export-Import Bank
U.S. International Development Cooperation Agency
U.S. International Trade Commission
U.S. Postal Service
Veterans Administration

SAMPLE OUTLINE

This outline covers the growth of the civil service. A chronological survey from its inception through its various changes and controversies reveals both the good and the bad sides of federal bureaucracies.

GROWTH AND CHANGE IN THE CIVIL SERVICE

I. President Washington set early precedents

A. "Fitness of Character" important

B. High officers changed with the new president

C. Civil servants held their jobs a long time

II. Late eighteenth and early nineteenth century—"government by gentlemen"

A. Jefferson upheld Washington's precedent

1. After 1800, Jeffersonians took control from Federalists
2. Jefferson kept moderate Federalists in the government

B. Many important employees served through several presidencies

1. Richard Cutts, Superintendent General of Military Supplies, 1815–1829
2. Abraham Bradley, Assistant Postmaster General, 1802–1829
3. Peter Hagner, Auditor and Clerk, 1792–1849

III. Andrew Jackson's spoils system makes changes necessary

A. Broke precedents assigning jobs

1. Used party loyalty
2. Used election campaign workers

B. A growing bureaucracy changed

1. Posts were bargained and dealt for
2. Government became a huge employer
    a. Occupied more of the president's time
    b. People began to view government as corrupt

IV. Several acts were instituted to correct problems

A. Pendleton Act of 1883

1. Two causes
    a. Garfield's assassination
    b. Reaction against corruption and scandals
2. Major changes
    a. Merit and ability designated as criteria
    b. Established civil service commission
    c. Covered about 10 percent of lower positions

B. Hatch Act of 1939

1. Banned civil servants from partisan political activity
2. Kept politicians from using civil service for political means

C. Civil Service Reform Act of 1978

1. Problems perceived in the civil service
    a. Incompetent workers not easily fired
    b. Automatic pay increases
    c. No incentive for good work
2. Jimmy Carter's Reform act made some changes
    a. Streamlined firing procedures
    b. Created Senior Executive Service
    c. Protected whistle-blowers

CHRONOLOGY

The Creation of Executive Departments

1789 The **Department of State**, headed by the secretary of state, handles relations with other nations.

1789 The **Department of War**, predecessor of the Department of Defense, was used to coordinate the armed forces.

1789 The **Department of Treasury**, headed by the secretary of the treasury, includes such responsibilities as minting U.S. currency and collecting taxes through the IRS.

1849 The **Department of the Interior**, headed by the secretary of the interior, is in charge of such things as parks, conservation, and land and power development.

1870 The **Department of Justice**, headed by the attorney general and including the FBI, deals with federal offenses.

1889 The **Department of Agriculture**, headed by the secretary of agriculture, tries to stabilize crops and prices and helps with agricultural research.

1913 The **Department of Commerce**, headed by the secretary of commerce, promotes domestic and foreign trade and transportation.

1913 The **Department of Labor**, headed by the secretary of labor, is concerned with helping workers by improving working conditions and wages and by creating new jobs.

1947 The **Department of Defense**, headed by the secretary of defense, replaces the Department of War and is in charge of the army, navy, marines, and air force.

1953 The **Department of Health, Education, and Welfare**, headed by the secretary of health, education, and welfare, covered all levels of education from elementary to college as well as Social Security, FDA, etc.

1965 The **Department of Housing and Urban Development**, headed by the secretary of housing and urban development, manages federal programs in order to improve housing and mass transit, generally in impoverished areas.

1966 The **Department of Transportation**, headed by the secretary of transportation, develops and coordinates national transportation policies and programs.

1977 The **Department of Energy**, headed by the secretary of energy, is responsible for research and conservation.

1979 The **Department of Education, and the Department of Health and Human Services** were created from the Department of Health, Education and Welfare.

SHORT READING LIST

Frederick C. Mosher, ed., *Basic Literature of American Public Administration, 1787–1950.* Includes some of the key essays and ideas concerning the development of the federal bureaucracy; great primary source readings on bureaucracy.

Anthony Downs, *Inside Bureaucracy*. Uses the common factors inherent in bureaucratic positions to explain the behavior, strengths, and weaknesses of bureaucrats.

Harold Seidman, *Politics, Position, and Power: The Dynamics of Federal Organization*, 3rd ed. Examines bureaucracy from varying perspectives.

Jeffrey L. Pressman and Aaron B. Wildavsky, *Implementation*. Shows the obstacles involved in implementing government policy.

Charles E. Linblom, *The Policy-Making Process*. Provides a brief, theoretical view of policy-making, with an emphasis on experts and their roles.

Herbert Kaufman, *Red Tape: Its Origins, Uses and Abuses*. Presents the problems of the bureaucracy as a microcosm of the problems of the larger society.

Frederick C. Mosher, *Democracy and Public Service*, 2nd ed. Analyzes the historic relationship between public service and political culture.

James Q. Mosher, *The Politics of Regulation*. Shows the pluses and minuses of regulation in several different areas.

Douglas Yates, *Bureaucratic Democracy: The Search for Democracy and Efficiency in American Government*. Analyzes bureaucracy in terms of democratic theory.

Chapter

Political Parties

MAJOR THEMES AND QUESTIONS

Development of Political Parties

1. Explain the First, Second, Third, Fourth, Fifth, and Sixth Party Eras.
2. Define the functions and purposes of a political party.
3. What accounts for the persistence of the two party system?
4. Describe Alexander Hamilton's Federalist party.
5. Contrast the Federalists to Thomas Jefferson's Democratic-Republican (Jeffersonian) party.
6. What accounts for the early demise of the Federalist party?
7. When was the only period in U.S. history with a single party?
8. What groups did Andrew Jackson's Democrats attract?
9. Who did the Whigs tend to represent?
10. How did slavery affect the Second Party Era?
11. What was the Know-Nothing party?
12. What alliance formed the Republican party, and what was the major issue of the early Republican party?
13. What similarities and differences exist between the early GOP and the modern Republican party?
14. Why is the election of Republican William McKinley considered a watershed in American political history?
15. Why did the Great Depression lead many Americans to become disenchanted with the Republican party?
16. Discuss why Americans have become more disenchanted with party affiliation since the 1980s.
17. What are the general differences between the Republican and Democratic parties?
18. What role have third parties played in American politics?
19. Why are political parties considered to be extraconstitutional?
20. What causes realignment?

ROAD MAP

Party Organization

1. Explain the danger of political patronage using the examples of Tammany Hall in New York City and Richard J. Daley of Chicago.
2. How does the party system complement the legal system in choosing public officials?
3. How do parties recruit and train political leaders?
4. What is a party platform?
5. How do parties raise and spend funds?
6. How does a party pick its national chairperson? What is the function of the chairperson?
7. Why does the expression "political machine" have negative connotations?
8. What are the coalitions within a party and how do they operate?
9. Is the party system destined to fall apart?
10. How has computer technology revitalized certain functions of political parties?

Parties and the People

1. What do members of the same party need to have in common?
2. To what extent does the modern Democratic party represent lower-income people, and the Republican party upper-income people?
3. Why has the Democratic party attracted greater minority support?
4. How can parties simplify the election process for voters?
5. How can parties make the government more responsible to the voters?
6. To what extent has the decrease in the patronage system and the spoils system weakened voters' attachment to parties?
7. How did early parties use neighborhood party welfare systems to help their own party?
8. From what early parties did the modern Democratic and Republican parties develop?

MAJOR TERMS AND CONCEPTS

Major and Third Parties

Whig
Federalist
Republican
Liberal Republican
Liberty
Democratic
National Democrat
Free Soil
Prohibition
Socialist
Progressive (La Follette)
Union
Socialist Workers
Greenback
People's (Populist)
Libertarian
U.S. Labor
Tory
Antifederalist
National Republican
Democratic Republican
American ("Know-Nothing")
Southern Democrats
States' Rights Democratic (Dixiecrat)
Socialist Labor

Constitutional Union
Communist
Progressive (Bull Moose)
Progressive (H. Wallace)
Anti-Mason
American Independent (G. Wallace)
Worker's World
National Unity
Citizens
Reform

Structure and Function

party system
two-party system
First Party System (Era)
Second Party System (Era)
Third Party System (Era)
Fourth Party System (Era)
Fifth Party System (Era)
Sixth Party System (Era)
decentralized system
realignment
majority election
fragmented elections
independents
state committee
party identification
gender gap
waning patronage
caucuses
public financing of campaigns
macing
socialization theory of partisan realignment
radical
left wing
liberal
moderate
radical left
plurality
closed primary
split-level realignment
responsible parties
at large
centrist
spoils system
plurality election
proportional election
platform
political machine
national committee
coalition
party decline
regulars
PAC (political action committee)
single-issue interest groups
referendum
dealignment
ward
party reform
independent voter
right wing
conservative
patronage
radical right
reactionary
pressure group
interest aggregation
consensus
merit employment
opposition party
"missionary party"
"broker party"
"loyal opposition"
"solid South"

SAMPLE OUTLINE

An extensively discussed trend of the last two decades has been the decline of the power and influence of the current two-party system. A good essay on this topic would have as its basic structure a description of the causes of party decline as well as an assessment of the negative and positive consequences of this decline.

THE DECLINE OF THE POWER AND INFLUENCE OF POLITICAL PARTIES

I. A variety of political, economic, and social factors have led to the decline

- A. Social causes
  - 1. Fewer people adopt the party of either parent
  - 2. Tarnished images of parties
    - a. Vietnam War
    - b. Watergate
    - c. Iran-Contra affair
    - d. Savings and Loan scandal
  - 3. Rise of the mass media
    - a. Diminishes the role of parties disseminating information
    - b. Allows a variety of candidates to reach a greater portion of the public
- B. Economic causes
  - 1. Public financing of campaigns
    - a. Federal Election Campaign Act of 1971
    - b. Candidates are less financially dependent on parties
  - 2. PACs support members of Congress
  - 3. Personal campaign organizations
    - a. Campaign workers are chosen by the candidate rather than the party
    - b. Organizations do their own fund-raising
  - 4. Public welfare system
    - a. Replaces informal party welfare system
    - b. People do not owe or depend on parties
- C. Political reasons
  - 1. Single-issue interest groups
    - a. Group members vote solely on that issue
    - b. Abortion and gun control are two controversial issues
  - 2. Primaries more important
    - a. Weaken influence of party regulars
    - b. Open conventions select candidates

II. Party decline has negative and positive aspects

- A. Negative aspects
  - 1. Elections are more confusing
    - a. Hard for parties to form a coalition
    - b. More candidates for each office
    - c. Each candidate has a personal platform

2. Power in government is not coordinated
    a. Government action needs coalitions
    b. Fractious elections make for a poorly coordinated government
3. Government is less responsive
    a. Individuals cannot put policies through by themselves
    b. No one group can be held responsible for the achievement or failure of stated goals

B. Positive aspects
1. System more democratic
    a. More "outside" group participation and influence
    b. Referendums bring issues straight to the voters
2. Communication gaps created can be overcome
    a. Television
    b. Computer
3. Changing times demand a flexible system
    a. U.S. society is more complex
    b. Parties should reflect this complexity

CHRONOLOGY

Important Third Parties in U.S. Politics

1840–48 The **Liberty** party wanted to abolish slavery.

1848–56 The **Free Soil** party wanted no slavery in any newly acquired territories, free homesteads for settlers, and an easier immigration process.

1856–60 The **American** or **Know-Nothing** party limited immigration, excluded foreigners and Catholics from public office, and required 21-year residency for citizenship.

1860–64 The **Constitutional Union** party wanted to preserve the union of states and the Constitution.

1869– The **Prohibition** party opposes the production, sale, and use of alcoholic beverages.

1876–84 The **Greenback** party wanted to have an increased money supply, an income tax, an eight-hour work day, and women's suffrage.

1892– The **Socialist Labor** party wants worker control of industry and a redistribution of wealth.

1891–96 The **People's** or **Populist** party wanted an increased money supply (free silver), the direct election of senators, and a graduated income tax.

1890– The **Socialist** party wants the collective ownership of production means, social security, and welfare legislation.

1912–16 **Roosevelt's Progressive** or **Bull Moose** party wanted government anti-trust action, women's suffrage, and minimum wage.

1924– The **American Communist** party wants an end to capitalism and a proletariat revolution with the power in the hands of the working class.

1924–46 **La Follette's Progressive** party wanted the breakup of corporate monopolies, farm relief, and reduced income taxes.

1948 The **States' Rights Democratic** or **Dixiecrat** party opposed a civil rights program.

1948–52 **Henry Wallace's Progressive** party wanted to strengthen civil rights laws and overturn Truman's anticommunist policies.

1968 The **American Independent** party supported restoring states' rights and opposed civil rights legislation.

1972– The **Libertarian** party wants to limit government influence in all aspects of American life.

SHORT READING LIST

V. O. Key, Jr., *Politics, Parties, and Pressure Groups.* This is a well-known text about the role of political parties in U.S. government.

Wilfred E. Binkley, *American Political Parties*, 4th ed. Presents a historical background of the current two-party system.

James L. Sundquist, *Dynamics of the Party System.* Centers around the idea of party realignment in historical context.

William Nisbet Chambers, Walter Dean Burnham, eds., *The American Party Systems: Stages of Political Development*, 2nd ed. Describes the party system from its inception to relatively recent times.

Everett Carl Ladd, *Where Have All the Voters Gone?,* 2nd ed. Gives an overview of the reasons for and possible consequences of the decline of political parties in the U.S.

Nelson W. Polsby, *Consequences of Party Reform.* Explores the pluses and minuses of recent party reforms.

Joseph Charles, *The Origins of the American Party System.* Uses political and social origins to discuss the party system as it stands today.

Chapter

Elections

MAJOR THEMES AND QUESTIONS

Campaigns

1. How has the increasing cost of running a campaign influenced elections?
2. What proportion of the average candidate's campaign funds is spent on the media?
3. What portion of the average candidate's campaign funds is supplied by political action committees?
4. Why must a candidate list contributions of over $200.00 with the Federal Election Commission (FEC)?
5. Why did Nixon's 1972 campaign incite the Federal Election Campaign Acts of 1971, 1974, and 1976?
6. What was the main purpose of the above-mentioned acts?
7. What limits have been set for total contributions to one campaign?
8. What are the arguments for and against having campaigns completely funded by the public?
9. Describe how successful wealthy candidates who have funded their own campaigns (*e.g.,* Nelson Rockefeller, Richard Ottinger, and Ross Perot) have been.
10. Can an election be bought?
11. How do taxpayers help fund campaigns?
12. What must a candidate do to receive federal matching funds?
13. What examples of negative campaigning can be found in the 1988 Bush campaign against Dukakis?
14. Select examples of negative campaigning from early elections (*e.g.*, Thomas Jefferson's opponents calling him the Antichrist, Grover Cleveland's opponents spreading rumors that he beat his wife and had illegitimate children, or Teddy Roosevelt's being labeled a drunkard and a drug fiend), and compare them to negative campaigning in modern elections. Has negative campaigning become more, or less, extreme?
15. Explain the quote from pollster Mark Mellman, "One of the fundamental facts of psychology is that negative information is processed more deeply than positive information" in terms of the rationale behind negative campaigns.
16. Discuss the direct primary as a means of nominating candidates.

ROAD MAP

- *Major Themes and Questions*
  - *Campaigns*
  - *Presidential Elections*
  - *Congressional Elections*
  - *Voters*
- *Major Terms and Concepts*
- *Sample Outline*
- *Chronology I*
- *Chronology II*
- *Short Reading List*

17. How is a closed primary run (as opposed to an open primary)?
18. Discuss the caucus and convention methods of selecting candidates.
19. What is a write-in candidate?
20. Is the nominating process more democratic than the election process?
21. Are campaigns too long and expensive?

Presidential Elections

1. What type of background has been common among presidential candidates?
2. How are delegates selected for the national convention, which nominates the presidential candidate?
3. How does the pool of delegates at the national convention differ from the voter pool? How might this influence the platform and ideas put forth by the candidates?
4. Why do party leaders prefer that one candidate have a clear majority of delegates going into the nominating convention as opposed to going through an open or brokered convention?
5. Compare the caucus method of delegate selection used by some states to the presidential preference primaries.
6. Describe the recent changes in the nomination process that have made it more democratic than it formerly was.
7. Explain how Vice President Hubert Humphrey managed to win the Democratic party's presidential nomination in 1968 without having entered a single primary, and how protests by anti-Vietnam War activists affected the election.
8. Why have the first caucus in Iowa and the first primary in New Hampshire come under such intense media scrutiny in recent election years?
9. What is "Super Tuesday" and what significance does it have in the nominating process?
10. Discuss different theories of the pluses and minuses of campaigning early.
11. Why was the electoral college system established?
12. How does the electoral college system work?
13. If problems such as faithless electors could hinder the democratic process, why is the electoral college system preserved?
14. What procedure is in place if no candidate wins a majority of the electoral votes?
15. Did the establishment of the electoral college indicate that the founders of the Constitution did not really have faith in the common person's ability to make decisions in a democratic system?
16. Using the elections of Rutherford B. Hayes and Benjamin Harrison, explain how it is possible to win the majority of the popular vote, but not win the electoral college vote.
17. Compare the retrospective voting model, the Michigan model, and the policy-oriented voter model to explain patterns in voting for presidential elections.
18. What role have televised debates had on presidential elections?
19. Explain the importance of the Kennedy-Nixon, Reagan-Carter, Dukakis-Bush, and Clinton-Bush-Perot debates to their respective campaigns.

Congressional Elections

1. What advantages does an incumbent have when running for Congress? How does it compare to the advantages of a presidential incumbent?
2. Why do House members from certain districts have a better chance than Senate members?
3. How does the franking privilege benefit congressional incumbents?
4. What influence does presidential popularity have in congressional elections?
5. What are the advantages and disadvantages of varying term lengths and staggered elections for members of Congress?

Voters

1. How effective was the Fifteenth Amendment (1870) in terms of extending voting privileges to black Americans?
2. How did Jim Crow laws limit black voting?
3. What was the purpose of a poll tax?
4. How did the grandfather clause in some restrictive southern states help poor, illiterate white voters?
5. How did white primaries in some states exclude blacks from the election process?
6. Explain the importance of the Nineteenth Amendment in terms of women's suffrage.
7. How did the Twenty-sixth Amendment broaden the electorate?
8. What is the purpose of the voter registration process required in most places in the United States?
9. How have the social characteristics of voters changed in recent times?
10. What accounts for the increase in political alienation on the part of voters?

MAJOR TERMS AND CONCEPTS

Getting Nominated

caucus method of delegate selection
Twenty-second Amendment
presidential election
candidates
party convention
credentials committee
running mate
"horse race"
dark horse
favorite son/daughter
party platform
political campaign
split ticket
straight ticket
primary
regional primary
closed primary
blanket primary
runoff primary
campaign fund
presidential preference
at large election
referendum
rules committee
platform committee
nominee
incumbency
keynote speech
endorsement

Campaign and Election Day

general election
bond election
gerrymandering
electoral college
franking privilege
recall
special election
single member district election
coattail effect
focus group
initiative
soft money
FECA
bond
safe seats
election reform
charisma
PACs
Twenty-third Amendment
negative campaigning
Buckley v. Valeo

Voting

female suffrage
literacy test
grandfather clause
Fifteenth Amendment
Twenty-sixth Amendment
voter turnout
low-stimulus elections
political alienation
political idealogy
minority-vote dilution
retrospective voting
absentee ballot
office-group ballot
residency
write-in candidate
poll watcher
vote fraud
bloc voting
Jim Crow
poll tax
white primary
Nineteenth Amendment
register
declining turnout
high-stimulus elections
selective perception
redistrict
minority-vote packing
Australian ballot
party-column ballot
precinct
bipartisan
plurality
recount
off-year election
franchise

SAMPLE OUTLINE

Every politician wishes that he/she could find a formula that would explain patterns in U.S. voting behavior. Many political scientists spend considerable energy trying to explain and predict voting habits. Voter turnout has dropped appreciably in the last 125 years, and is lower in the United States than in many other democracies. An essay about the U.S. voter can be written from many points of view. This outline first presents a profile of the characteristics of likely voters, and then offers some theories as to why people in the U.S. do or do not vote.

VOTER BEHAVIOR IN THE U.S.

I. There are certain characteristics shared by likely voters in the U.S.

A. Formally educated people are more likely to vote
1. College graduates make up the highest percentage of voters
2. People with some college education are the next highest
3. About half of high school graduates vote
4. Fewer than half of those who did not complete high school vote

B. Higher-income people are more likely to vote
1. Of those in the top fifth in family income, over 90 percent vote
2. Likeliness to vote steadily decreases as income level decreases

C. Whites are more likely to vote than minorities
1. Well over 50 percent of whites vote (the highest percentage)
2. About half of the black population votes
3. Fewer than 50 percent of Hispanics vote (the lowest percentage)

II. There are three main theories that explain voting behavior in the U.S.

A. Policy-oriented voter
1. Voters perceive differences in candidates according to policies
   a. Candidates are associated with foreign policy
   b. Single-issue voting on the rise
2. Many experts have problems with this theory
   a. Candidates are often unclear on issues
   b. Voters know little about candidates' position on issues

B. Michigan model
1. Developed by University of Michigan scholars
2. Voters respond to several factors
   a. Candidate's style
   b. Party loyalty
   c. Voters' perceptions
   d. Leadership abilities

C. Retrospective voting model
1. Voters look at incumbent candidate's past performance
2. Performance is more important than promises

III. Reasons for declining turnout

1. Widespread voter registration
2. Disaffection with political system
   a. Poor
   b. Minorities
   c. Uneducated
3. Decreasing partisanship
4. Satisfaction with status quo

CHRONOLOGY I

Supreme Court Cases Concerning Suffrage and Elections

1880 Ex parte Siebold allowed the conviction of an election commissioner, who violated both state and federal laws by stuffing the ballot box, to stand.

1915 *Guinn v. United States* voided an amendment to the Oklahoma constitution which contained a grandfather clause that required a literacy test for all except a specified group of voters. This group included those who were eligible to vote as of January 1, 1866, those who then resided in a foreign nation, and the descendants of such people.

1941 *United States v. Classic* allowed the conviction of a Louisiana election officer who perpetrated frauds in a primary election; ex parte Siebold was cited. The Court ruled "Where the state law has made the primary an integral part of the procedure of choice, or where in fact the primary effectively controls the choice, the right of the elector to have his ballot counted at the primary is likewise included in the rights protected by Article I, section 2."

1946 *Colegrove v. Green* declared that the Supreme Court could not become involved in a reapportionment problem in Illinois because it involved partisan politics, and the Constitution gave Congress authority in such matters.

1915–53 **Texas Primary Cases**: *Nixon v. Herndon* (1927) invalidated a law of the Texas legislature because the law excluded blacks from primary elections of the Democratic party. *Nixon v. Condon* (1932), *Grovey v. Townsend* (1935), *Smith v. Allwright* (1944), and *Terry v. Adams* (1953) all dealt with the problem of exclusive primaries, which usually decided the elections.

1964 *Wesberry v. Sanders* overruled *Colegrove v. Green* on the grounds that, since every voter is equal, then congressional districts must be apportioned as equally as possible.

1964 *Harper v. Virginia State Board of Elections* did away with the poll tax once and for all.

1966 *South Carolina v. Katzenbach* upheld provisions of the **Federal Voting Rights Act of 1965**.

1970 *Oregon v. Mitchell* upheld the constitutionality of an amendment to the 1965 **Voting Rights Act**. This case resulted in state legislatures extending suffrage to 18-year-olds, which was later incorporated in the Twenty-sixth Amendment (1971).

1976 *Buckley v. Valeo* invalidated some parts of the **Federal Election Campaign Acts of Congress**, 1971–1974. This decision waived the limits of what a candidate or group can spend on an election, but maintained the limits for contributors.

CHRONOLOGY II

Expanding Voting Rights

1790–1850 **Property qualifications** for voters are dropped by states.

1869 Wyoming territory grants suffrage to women.

1870 Black people get the right to vote from the **Fifteenth Amendment**. **Jim Crow laws** exclude black voters in southern states.

1920 Women get the right to vote in state and federal elections from the **Nineteenth Amendment.**

1944 *Smith v. Allwright* results in the Supreme Court ban of **white primaries**.

1964 **Poll tax** is banned by the **Twenty-fourth Amendment**.

1965 **Literacy test** for those with at least a sixth-grade education is waived by the **Voting Rights Act**.

1971 Citizens 18 and older are given the right to vote by the **Twenty-sixth Amendment**.

1982 Requires states to redistrict in such a way that majority-minority representation is ensured.

SHORT READING LIST

Herbert Asher, *Presidential Elections and American Politics*, 3rd ed. Analyzes the way in which Americans have selected candidates.

Angus Campbell, Philip E. Converse, Warren E. Miller, and Donald E. Stokes, *The American Voter*. This classic work explores campaigns and elections from the voter's point of view. It is based on surveys taken in the 1950s.

Norman Nie, Sidney Verba, and John Petrocik, *The Changing American Voter*. This work is similar to *The American Voter*; it uses later data from the 1960s and 1970s.

Raymond Wolfinger and Steven Rosenstone, *Who Votes?* Studies voter turnout.

Benjamin I. Page, *Choices and Echoes in Presidential Elections*. Analyzes how candidates' actions influence the voters during elections.

Nelson W. Polsby and Aaron B. Wildavsky, *Presidential Elections*. This is a general study of the process of electing a president.

Theodore H. White, *The Making of the President 1960*. Gives a famous account of what really happened during the 1960 presidential election.

Herbert E. Alexander, *Financing Politics: Money, Elections, and Political Reform*, 2nd ed. Provides an authoritative text on the topic of campaign finance.

Benjamin Ginsberg, *Consequences of Consent: Elections, Citizen Control, and Popular Acquiescence*. Examines political campaigns within the larger framework of their relationship to and influence on society.

Public Opinion Magazine. Gives good, current information on elections and campaigns.

Mark R. Levy and Michael S. Kramer, *The Ethnic Factor: How America's Minorities Decide Elections*. Discusses the importance of minorities as swing votes in elections; much of the research is based on the 1972 election.

William R. Keech and Donald R. Matthews, *The Party's Choice*. Concentrates on the presidential nomination process from 1940 to 1976.

Gary Jacobson, *Money in Congressional Elections*. Discusses the influence of money on congressional campaigns.

Richard S. Katz and Kevin S. Mulcahy, *America Votes*. Interprets the significance of elections.

Chapter

Political Socialization

MAJOR THEMES AND QUESTIONS

Gaining Political Knowledge

1. What does the term *political socialization* mean, and how does it come about?
2. Discuss the importance of family, school, peer groups, and the media as agents of political socialization.
3. Why are many Americans apathetic toward many political issues?
4. What does the term *attentive public* describe?
5. What would constitute a crisis in the political legitimacy of government, in terms of lack of public approval and/or interest?
6. What is the relationship between political efficacy, both internal (an individual's evaluation of his/her ability to influence policy) and external (an individual's assessment of governmental responsiveness), and participation by citizens in government?
7. How does transfer theory explain Americans' attitudes toward their leaders?
8. What importance do textbooks have in the development of political thought?
9. To what extent does television "nationalize" U.S. culture?

Media and the Government

1. Why do some refer to the media as the "fifth branch" of government?
2. Why does the Constitution make specific provisions for the media in the First Amendment, saying "Congress shall make no law. . . abridging the freedom . . . of the press"?
3. What role did the press play in the early years of U.S. government?
4. Explain the significance of Justice Felix Frankfurter's (1939–1962) statement, "A free press is indispensable to the workings of our democratic society."
5. What limits are put on the press by the Constitution?
6. Compare the limits put on press coverage during the Vietnam War as opposed to the Persian Gulf War. Were the Persian Gulf War restrictions justified?
7. What is the White House News Summary?
8. What types of early media regulation existed in the hands of the Department of Congress?
9. What powers did the Federal Radio Commission, established in 1927, have?

ROAD MAP

10. The Federal Communications Commission (FCC) was established in 1934. Explain its function and authority.
11. In the past few decades, has the FCC moved toward more or less regulation?
12. How has the equal-time rule, established in the Communications Act of 1934, influenced political campaigns?
13. How important is it for a president to maintain good relations with the media?
14. Compare the different ways in which Presidents Kennedy, Nixon, Carter, and Bush handled the media.
15. Discuss the influence of investigative reporting in terms of the Watergate scandal.
16. Discuss the role press secretaries and media specialists play for elected officials.
17. How do public officials use media leaks to influence the course of events in government? Discuss the confirmation hearing of Supreme Court Justice Clarence Thomas as an example.
18. To what extent does and should the media serve as a source of information to the government in domestic and international affairs?

Media and the Public

1. Although journalists are not elected, they do have a large impact on the government. Describe some methods which could discourage poor journalistic work.
2. How did the media influence public opinion during the Vietnam War?
3. How influential have such media figures as Walter Cronkite, Johnny Carson, and Dan Rather been in forming public opinion?
4. To what extent is media image important to the popularity of an elected official? Are "good-looking" officials more likely to be popular?
5. Discuss the media as vehicles of communication.
6. Discuss the media's role as a "gatekeeper" that decides what information the public will be privy to.
7. Explain how the First Amendment's guarantee of freedom of the press was affected by the 1972 *Branzburg v. Hayes* decision and the subsequent shield laws enacted by individual states.
8. What are some concerns of public officials regarding the ever-shortening "sound bites" used on the evening television news?
9. What truth is there in former Vice President Spiro Agnew's statement, "A small group of men, numbering perhaps no more than a dozen anchormen, commentators, and executive producers settle upon the film and commentary that is to reach the public."
10. Is it more accurate to say that the media shape public opinion, or that public opinion decides what the media present?

Public Opinion

1. Which factors in American public opinion are constant, and which are dynamic?
2. How did George Gallup revolutionize poll taking?
3. Explain how closed-ended and open-ended questions are used to obtain information in polls.

4. How have opinion polls been wrong in the past? Use Harry S. Truman's 1948 victory over Thomas E. Dewey as an example.
5. How have politicians come to rely on polls both during elections and while in office?

Political Ideology

1. Explain classical liberalism as it was practiced by Thomas Jefferson and Andrew Jackson.
2. How does Andrew Jackson's struggle against the wealth and power of a national bank exemplify classical liberalism?
3. How did Vice President Bush use the label "liberal" against his opponent Michael Dukakis in the 1988 presidential campaign?
4. In what way was populism a variation of liberalism?
5. How was progressivism related to classical liberalism?
6. Describe the neoliberal movement of the 1980s and 1990s.
7. Explain early conservatism as expounded by Edmund Burke and John Adams.
8. Why do conservatives embrace laissez faire economics?
9. What are the cornerstones of contemporary conservatism expounded by Barry Goldwater?
10. Describe the democratic socialist movement as it was envisioned by Eugene V. Debs.
11. In what ways have libertarian ideas influenced the major parties?
12. How do race, social class, religion, and generation tend to affect political ideology?

MAJOR TERMS AND CONCEPTS

Regulations and Restrictions

First Amendment
Department of Commerce
Communications Act of 1934, Section 13
Branzburg v. Hayes
Federal Communications Commission
Federal Radio Commission
equal-time rule
fairness doctrine
shield laws

Media Terms

journalist
mass media
press conference
press secretary
press release
media bias
communication vehicle
media as a gatekeeper
area of dominant influence (ADI)
network news anchor
fifth branch
news summary
leak
censorship
wire service
media as talent scout
backgrounders
photo opportunities
Nielsen ratings

Political Ideology

classical liberal
neoliberal
moderate
"far right"
reactionary
laissez faire

Brookings Institution
Heritage Foundation
progressive
democratic socialism
social Darwinism
Hubert Humphrey
Woodrow Wilson
Thomas Jefferson
Herbert Croly
Barry Goldwater
Eugene V. Debs
conservative
neoconservative
centrist
"far left"
think tank
Americans for Democratic Action
American Enterprise Institute
populism
new right
libertarianism
Andrew Jackson
Theodore Roosevelt
John Adams
Edmund Burke
William Graham Sumner
William F. Buckley, Jr.
Ed Clarke

Public Opinion

status quo
peer groups
political culture
political socialization
political symbols
straw polls
sampling
sampling error
quota sample
attentive public
internal political efficacy
external political efficacy
political efficacy
survey results
George Gallup
closed-ended research
leading question
transfer theory
party identification
cluster sampling
random sample
biased sample
agents of socialization
gender gap
probability
political legitimacy
survey research
questionnaire
open-ended research
social learning theory
cognitive development theory
rational actor model

SAMPLE OUTLINE

If one acknowledges the importance of the media to the functioning of the government, then a natural concern is the media's fairness. Both government officials and regular citizens have at time criticized the media for being biased. This outline breaks the topic down into several parts: how the media chooses what news it will present to the public, famous accusations of press bias, and disputes against press bias.

MEDIA BIAS

I. Factors that go into choosing stories for the evening news

A. Newsworthiness
1. Disasters
2. Political turning points
3. "Scoops"

B. Economic factors
1. Limited reporters, camera crews, etc.
2. Many reporters are located in Washington, D.C., resulting in many Washington stories
3. Nielsen ratings: news must attract viewers

C. Preferences of news editors and reporters
1. Strive for objectivity
2. Personal views cannot be totally eliminated
   a. Choice of stories
   b. Spin put on story

II. Evidence of media bias

A. Nixon-Agnew administration complained of liberal bias
1. Agnew said a tiny group of journalists were responsible for influencing public opinion
2. Agnew called the press "nattering nabobs of negativism"
3. Nixon had frequent confrontational exchanges with the press
4. *Washington Post* found evidence to cause Nixon's and Agnew's resignations

B. Studies show bias against Carter in 1980
1. Majority of coverage was negative
2. Reagan received more positive coverage

C. Republicans claim unfair "Quayle bashing"
1. Quayle pointed to liberals controlling media
2. Quayle was a popular topic of media ridicule

III. Arguments against media bias

A. The higher-level new editors tend to be more conservative than reporters

B. Reporters like scandals, regardless of party affiliation
1. Nixon and Agnew—Republican
2. Gary Hart—Democratic
3. Iran-Contra—Republican
4. Clinton affair allegations—Democratic

C. The public has a wide choice of news sources
1. Cable TV has provided a huge variety of news
   a. Full coverage of Congress
   b. 24-hour news
2. Wide choice has enabled viewers to become more sophisticated

CHRONOLOGY I

Important Events in the Political Development of Radio and Television

1923 A broader audience was able to listen simultaneously to President Calvin Coolidge's opening address to Congress when **telephone links** were used.

1927 The **Federal Radio Commission** was created not only to ensure private ownership of the radio industry but also to establish federal controls.

1933 The first **"fireside chat"** was delivered by President Franklin Roosevelt, further promoting the radio as a tool of direct communication.

1934 The **Federal Communications Commission (FCC)** replaced the Federal Radio Commission. Congress created it, sensitive to the needs of the burgeoning television and movie industries.

1940 The Republican and Democratic conventions were televised for the first time.

1951 The Supreme Court rules that movies are protected under the First Amendment.

1952 Richard Nixon's **"Checkers speech"** helped salvage his political career.

1960 The presidential debate between Nixon and Kennedy was the first ever to be televised.

1962 Kennedy announced the **Cuban Missile Crisis** to the world via a television broadcast from the Oval Office, effectively using television as a political and public-relations tool.

1963 **Network evening news** expanded to a 30-minute format from what was previously a 15-minute format.

1964 Network television broadcast the results of the Johnson-Goldwater presidential election before California polls had closed.

1965–71 **Walter Cronkite** rose in national prominence as a CBS anchorman during the Vietnam War, which was the first war to be extensively covered via satellite.

1979 The House of Representatives approved television coverage.

1986 The Senate approved television coverage.

1988 George Bush ran a highly effective **negative television campaign** against his presidential opponent Michael Dukakis.

CHRONOLOGY II

Development of Liberal and Conservative Movements in the U.S.

1690 Liberal: John Locke's *Second Treatise on Government* influenced many classical liberal founding fathers.

1776 Liberal: Adam Smith's *Wealth of Nations* and Thomas Paine's *Common Sense* both propounded liberal views.

1790 Conservative: Edmund Burke's *Reflections on the French Revolution* criticized the liberal excesses of the revolution; it was influential in the U.S.

1851 Conservative: Herbert Spencer's *Social Statistics* illustrated his laissez faire views.

1883 Conservative: William Graham Sumner's *What Social Classes Owe to Each Other* propounded conservative views.

1892 Liberal: Convention for the first **Populist** party was held.

1896 Liberal: Much of the Populist party platform was adopted by the Democratic party.

1913–16 Liberal: President Woodrow Wilson promoted progressivism with his **New Freedom** program.

1920 Conservative: Warren Harding's election to president hailed a conservative era in government.

1933–36 Liberal: FDR's **New Deal** created a heretofore unseen level of government involvement in citizens' lives.

1955 Conservative: the *National Review*, an important conservative and intellectual magazine, was published.

1964 Liberal: Congress passed the **Civil Rights Act**.

1964 Conservative: The Republican party selected **Barry Goldwater** as its candidate for president, strengthening ties between Republicans and Conservatives.

1965 Liberal: President Johnson's **Great Society** legislation was passed.

1980 Conservative: Ronald Reagan was elected president and used his mandate to promote conservative policies.

1988 Conservative: Republicans used the term "liberal" negatively to help defeat Democrats.

CHRONOLOGY III

Supreme Court Cases Affecting the Press

1931 *Near v. Minnesota* declared unconstitutional a state law that prevented a local newspaper from stridently attacking the integrity of police officials. The Court decided that the law constituted censorship, and thus violated the basic right of freedom of the press.

1936 *Grosjean v. American Press Co.* invalidated a Louisiana state law which imposed what the Court felt were unfair taxes on newspaper advertisements with political views in opposition to those of Governor Huey P. Long.

1964 *New York Times Co. v. Sullivan* reversed a decision by Alabama courts that had awarded heavy damages to law enforcement officers who sued *The Times* over an unfavorable paid political advertisement it had published. The Court stated that "debate on public issues should be uninhibited, robust, and wide open."

1974 *Branzburg v. Hayes* weakened the right to confidentiality, saying that there were times when a reporter must testify and reveal the contents of his/her notebooks.

1974 *Miami Herald Publishing Co. v. Tormillo* weakened a Florida statute guaranteeing equal rights to free space in the press, saying that it would inhibit a newspaper's right of free speech to require it to pay for the space of those who hold contrary opinions to the paper.

1976 *Nebraska Press Association v. Stuart* struck down a state court order which had stopped the press from publishing pre-trial confessions of accused persons.

1976 *Time, Inc. v. Firestone* upheld a jury verdict which had found *Time* magazine guilty of misrepresenting the facts in a divorce case.

1978 *Zurcher v. The Stamford Daily* sustained the right to issue a search warrant against a student newspaper which law enforcement officials felt had incriminating photographs revealing the identity of demonstrators.

SHORT READING LIST

Roy C. Macridis, *Contemporary Political Ideologies*, 2nd ed. Provides a broad overview of different political ideologies.

Walter E. Volkomer, ed., *The Liberal Tradition in American Thought*. Provides important historical readings on liberalism.

Jay Sigler, ed., *The Conservative Tradition in American Thought*. Provides important historical readings on conservatism.

Walter Lippman, *Public Opinion*. This is one of the earliest studies on public opinion.

Ronald Berkman and Laura W. Kitch, *Politics in the Media Age*. Gives a general overview of the influence of the media on politics.

Austin Ranney, *The Impact of Television on American Politics*. Concentrates on the role of television in politics.

John R. MacArthur, *Second Front*. Deals with the topic of censorship and propaganda in the Persian Gulf War. It examines the development of the Defense Department's use of public relations to avoid the problems faced by negative coverage by the press during the Vietnam War.

Doris A. Graber, *Mass Media and American Politics*. Analyzes research done in the area of media influence on politics.

V. O. Key, Jr., *Public Opinion and American Democracy*. Combines information on how public opinion is formulated with popular ideas on what a democracy requires in terms of public awareness.

Chapter

Interest Groups and Lobbying

MAJOR THEMES AND QUESTIONS

History of and Theory Behind Public Participation in Democracy

1. What advantages does collective participation in a democracy have over individual participation?
2. Using the following quote by James Madison, taken from *Federalist No. 10*, explain what negative aspect of interest groups is being inferred, and what solution to the problems created by a large variety of interests groups is being offered: "A zeal for different opinions concerning religion, concerning government, and many other points...have, in turn, divided mankind into parties, inflamed them with mutual animosity, and rendered them much more disposed to view and oppress each other than to cooperate for the common good.... The regulation of these various and interfering interests forms the principal task of modern legislation and involves the spirit of party and faction in the necessary and ordinary operations of government."
3. Is the U.S. society closer to a pluralist or an elitist society?
4. How did lobbying begin during Ulysses S. Grant's presidency?
5. Explain the criticism that the precedent set to select minorities and women to federal courts goes against the original intention of the courts being separate from politics. What is the view of related interest groups towards the subject?
6. What role did the NAACP play in the landmark *Brown v. Board of Education of Topeka* Supreme Court case?
7. Explain how free-rider barriers, material incentives, and purposive incentives relate to people's motivation for joining interest groups.
8. Explain the concept of proximity of interest groups in terms of salience, transmission of standards, and legitimacy.
9. Why are interest groups considered to be part of the "iron triangle" of politics?
10. What is interest group gridlock?

ROAD MAP

- *Major Themes and Questions*
  - *History of and Theory Behind Public Participation in Democracy*
  - *Interest Groups*
  - *Strategies for Influencing Public Policy*
- *Major Terms and Concepts*
- *Sample Outline*
- *Chronology*
- *Short Reading List*

Interest Groups

1. What is a latent interest group? Which latent interest groups are most important in U.S. politics?
2. When is an interest group labeled "reactionary" and/or "radical"?
3. Why is the lobbying done by various chambers of commerce on behalf of business considered to be grass-roots lobbying?
4. What is the difference between the National Association of Manufacturers and the National Federation of Independent Business?
5. What has been the general trend in the effectiveness of labor unions as lobbyists?
6. How has Ralph Nader successfully developed an influential consumer-advocacy group?
7. What do professional groups like the AMA do for their members in terms of influencing public policy?
8. What role do racial and ethnic groups like the NAACP, CORE, LULAC, and AIM play in U.S. politics?
9. Discuss the ups and downs of conservative religious groups like the Moral Majority and their forays into politics.
10. What is a single-issue interest group?
11. Discuss the modern political action committees that formed in the 1970s.

Strategies for Influencing Public Policy

1. How have political action committees circumvented the limits that exist for contributions to political campaigns?
2. The motto "Elect Your Friends, Defeat Your Enemies" is prevalent among interest groups. What is its significance?
3. Why have former government officials been able to get high-paying jobs as lobbyists after leaving public office? Why are some people concerned with the ethics of former officials becoming lobbyists?
4. What are some benefits of the direct mail method of influencing public opinion, and how have computers affected this method?
5. How did the Federal Election Act of 1974 indirectly lead to the proliferation of PACs?
6. How do interest groups involve themselves in the judicial process?
7. What is the purpose of an amicus curiae brief?
8. Describe grass-roots lobbying.

MAJOR TERMS AND CONCEPTS

Important Interest Groups

American Federation of Labor-Congress of Industrial Organizations (AFL-CIO)
Association of Manufacturers
American Iron and Steel Institute
American Farm Bureau Federation
National Farmers Association (NFO)
National Organization for Women (NOW)
Moral Majority
United States Catholic Conference
Political Action Committee (PAC)
Christian Right
National Right to Life Committee
National Rifle Association (NRA)

Public Interest Research Group (PIRG)
International Ladies Garment Workers Union (ILGWU)
Committee on Political National Education (COPE)
Chamber of Commerce
American Gas Association
American Medical Association (AMA)
American Agricultural Movement (AAM)
National Association for the Advancement of Colored People (NAACP)
Jewish Defense League (JDL)
National Conservative Political Action Committee (NCPAC)
Common Cause
American Civil Liberties Union (ACLU)
Americans for Democratic Action (ADA)
National Association of Manufacturers
National Education Association (NEA)
Sierra Club
National Association for Government Employees
National Grange
National Congress of American Indians
National Catholic Conference
American Jewish Committee
Progressive Political Action Committee (PROPAC)
American Bar Association (ABA)
International Brotherhood of Teamsters
National Audubon Society
League of Women Voters
League of United Latin American Citizens
National Alliance of Senior Citizens

Interest Group and Lobbying Terms

interest group
latent interest group
pluralism
lobbyist
salience
legitimacy
radical
opinion leaders
Federal Election Act of 1974
iron triangle
grass-roots lobbying
single-issue group
interest group gridlock
pluralist democracy
elitism
proximity
transmission of standards
reactionary
direct mail
influencing public policy
Federalist No. 10
subpoenas
amicus curiae brief
right-to-life movement
issue network
"citizen's lobby"
"problem of the powerless"
craft union
electioneering
cross-cutting cleavage
faction
industrial union
class-action suit
free-rider barrier to group membership
purposive incentives to group membership
material incentives to group membership
solidarity incentives to group membership

SAMPLE OUTLINE

This outline deals with the way interest groups influence government policy. Since this is a relatively broad topic, the keys to writing a good essay are selectivity and organization. This outline selects and breaks down some of the most important topics.

INTEREST GROUPS INFLUENCING GOVERNMENT POLICY

I. Creating grass-roots pressure for change

- A. Legislators respond to constituency pressures
- B. Media is a majority conduit
  - 1. Paid advertisements
    - a. Television
    - b. Newspaper
    - c. Radio
  - 2. Direct mailings
- C. Without grass-roots support, an interest group loses credibility

II. Electioneering for change

- A. Group's leader urges members to endorse sympathetic candidates
- B. Political action committees
  - 1. Raise and distribute money
  - 2. Raised $350 million for 1987–88 election cycle
  - 3. High cost of elections make them important
    - a. Difficult to win without PAC sponsored commercials
    - b. Many candidates are likely to conform platform to PAC acceptability
  - 4. Usually support incumbents because PACs prefer winners

III. Lobbying for change

- A. Professional lobbyists visit legislators' offices
- B. Provide information
  - 1. Legislators sometimes have limited resources to investigative problems
  - 2. Lobbyists can supply research that supports their own cause
- C. Washington insiders are often hired to lobby
- D. Basic idea of lobbying is to persuade

IV. Using the judicial process for change

- A. Can affect selection of judges
- B. Suits filed by interest groups (these are often class-action suits)
- C. Interest groups support individuals to bring legal action
  - 1. Lend financial and legal support
  - 2. NAACP's role in *Brown v. Board of Education of Topeka*
- D. Amicus curiae briefs to show supporting opinions
- E. Lobby court members

CHRONOLOGY

Founding of Influential Interest Groups

1847 The **American Medical Association** sets standards for medical schools and hospitals and represents medical professionals in Congress.

1857 The **National Education Association** works to improve the quality of education in general and to increase teachers' salaries.

1867 The **National Grange** helps rural families through legislation, higher price supports, and self-help.

1878 The **American Bar Association** supports and maintains standards for lawyers and judges.

1892 The **Sierra Club** tries to preserve wilderness areas.

1895 The **National Association of Manufacturers** represents mainly large business interests.

1902 The **National Farmers Union** lobbies for higher government price supports for crops and livestock.

1903 The **International Brotherhood of Teamsters** represents groups like truck-drivers and dock workers.

1905 The **National Audubon Society** promotes conservation of land and wildlife.

1906 The **American Jewish Committee** protects the religious and civil rights of Jewish Americans.

1909 The **National Association for the Advancement of Colored People (NAACP)** works to obtain civil rights for African Americans.

1912 The **Chamber of Commerce of the United States** represents mainly small-business interests.

1919 The **American Farm Bureau Federation** promotes free trade and opposes price support for farmers.

1920 The **League of Women Voters** educates the public on political matters, sponsors political forums such as debates, and promotes participation in government.

1920 The **American Civil Liberties Union** tries to protect the basic freedoms guaranteed in the Bill of Rights.

1929 The **League of United Latin American Citizens** supports civil rights for Hispanic Americans.

1944 The **National Congress of American Indians** works to protect the resources and rights of Native Americans.

1955 The **American Federation of Labor-Congress of Industrial Organizations (AFL-CIO)** supports the interests of lower-skilled wage earners.

1961 The **National Association of Government Employees** represents the interests of mainly low-level government employees.

1966 The **National Organization for Women (NOW)** works to end sexual discrimination against women.

1970 The **Common Cause** promotes citizens' involvement in government.

1972 The **Business Roundtable** has the general purpose of promoting business interests and acting as a "think tank" on business' behalf.

1974 The **National Alliance of Senior Citizens** lobbies Congress on behalf of senior citizens.

1979 The **Moral Majority** promoted traditional conservative values. (This group no longer exists.)

SHORT READING LIST

James Madison, *Federalist No. 10*. Remains one of the most important essays on the theory behind citizen participation in government.

David Truman, *The Governmental Process*. Another classic account of the role of public interest groups in the general context of government.

Elizabeth Drew, *Politics and Money*. Criticizes the use of money to influence politicians.

Robert A. Dahl, *Who Governs?* Succinctly describes the role of interest groups in American pluralist democracy.

Theodore Lowi, *The End of Liberalism*. Criticizes interest groups for mainly promoting liberalism.

Mancur Olson, *The Rise and Decline of Nations*. Examines the conflicts that naturally arise in pluralistic societies.

Mancur Olson, *The Logic of Collective Action*. Explains the formation of interest groups in terms of economic forces.

Raymond A. Bauer, Ithiel de Sola Pool, and Lewis A. Dexter, *American Business and Public Policy*. Examines the strong influence that business and industry hold over Congress.

Kay Lehman Schlozman and John Tierney, *Organized Interests and American Democracy*. Provides a general overview of over 175 interest groups that wield influence in Washington.

Chapter

Civil Liberties and Civil Rights

MAJOR THEMES AND QUESTIONS

Constitutional Guarantees to Civil Liberties

1. What civil liberties were protected in Article 1, section 9, of the Constitution? Include bill of attainder, *ex post facto* law, and habeas corpus in your discussion.
2. In what way is the definition of treason, found in Article 3, section 3 also a guarantee of civil liberties?
3. In what way does Article 4 protect civil liberties by forbidding the use of a religious test as a qualification for national office?
4. Why is the following passage from the Fourteenth Amendment considered to be crucial to American civil liberties: "No State shall make or enforce any law which shall abridge the privileges or immunities of citizens of the United States; nor shall any State deprive any person of life, liberty, or property, without due process of law; nor deny to any person within its jurisdiction the equal protection of the laws"?
5. Discuss *Gitlow v. New York* and the "selective incorporation of the Bill of Rights."
6. Discuss *Palko v. Connecticut* in terms of "selective incorporation of the Bill of Rights" and protection from double jeopardy.
7. Why does the Constitution prohibit both *ex post facto* laws and bills of attainder?
8. How does the exclusionary rule created by judges strengthen the Fourth Amendment?
9. Discuss *Miranda v. Arizona* in terms of Fifth Amendment protection from coerced confessions.
10. How did the Sixth Amendment make the contest between the state and individual more equal?
11. Discuss the Eighth Amendment's prohibition of "cruel and unusual punishments" and its application to convicts sentenced to death.
12. Explain the significance of the Ninth Amendment, which states: "The enumeration in the Constitution, of certain rights, shall not be construed to deny or disparage others retained by the people."

ROAD MAP

History and Development of Civil Liberties

1. How has the Court decided upon the limits of free speech? Discuss the clear-and-present-danger and bad-tendency tests.
2. What were the ramifications of the Smith Act and subsequent Supreme Court rulings concerning this act?
3. How has obscenity been defined by the Supreme Court?
4. Discuss aid to sectarian schools and prayer in public schools in terms of how they have been handled by the government as civil liberties issues.
5. How has the presumption of innocence served the civil liberties of the accused?
6. Was the Solomon Amendment a bill of attainder?
7. What backlash has there been from victims who feel that accused criminals have too many rights and protections?
8. How have services like the Legal Services Corporation and pro bono lawyers helped protect the civil liberties of those accused of crimes?
9. Contrast Justice William O. Douglas's defense of individual rights to Chief Justice William H. Rehnquist's defense of majority rule.
10. What civil liberty issues are at stake in the controversy surrounding *Roe v. Wade*?
11. Discuss the Supreme Court's double standard in terms of its priorities in selected cases.
12. What are due process of law, substantive due process, and procedural due process?

The Development of Civil Rights

1. What have been some of the disputes over different definitions of equality? Include in your answer the equality of result, equality of opportunity, and equality of condition.
2. What are the moderate scrutiny test, reasonable basis test, and strict scrutiny test?
3. Discuss early racial discrimination in terms of slavery, the Emancipation Proclamation, the Thirteenth Amendment, and Reconstruction.
4. What role have organizations like the NAACP and the Legal Defense Fund played in the improvement of civil rights for African Americans?
5. Why is *Brown v. Board of Education of Topeka* considered a landmark decision?
6. What problems did the Civil Rights Act of 1964 address?
7. What are de jure segregation and de facto segregation?
8. What is affirmative action and why has it been criticized by some for promoting "reverse discrimination"?
9. Describe the importance of *The Regents of the University of California v. Bakke* in terms of its effect upon affirmative action.
10. What was accomplished by the Voting Rights Act of 1965? What change was made in this act in 1982?
11. What is "comparable worth"?
12. What have been some goals of the National Organization for Women (NOW)?
13. What is the Equal Rights Amendment and what have been some obstacles to its passage?
14. What argument have Native Americans often used when suing to reclaim land?
15. What explains the relatively weak impact that Hispanics and Asians have had in their quest for civil rights?

16. What civil rights problem does the minority business set-aside address?
17. Describe the suspect classification doctrine.
18. What are minority-vote dilution and minority-vote packing?
19. To what extent has civil disobedience affected the civil rights movement, and what precedents were set for civil disobedience in the founding of this country?

MAJOR TERMS AND CONCEPTS

Civil Liberties

ACLU
bad-tendency test
bill of attainder
capital punishment
civil liberties
criminal procedure
double jeopardy
due process of law
ex post facto law
Fourteenth Amendment
friend-of-the-court brief
immunity from prosecution
legal guilt
Lemon test
Magna Carta
misdemeanor
petit jury
presumption of innocence
amicus curiae
bail
Bill of Rights
civil punishment
clear-and-present-danger rule
cruel and unusual punishment
double standard
exclusionary rule
establishment clause
free-exercise clause
grand jury
information
Legal Services Corporation
libel
Miranda warnings
obscenity
presentment
prior restraint
Privacy Act
Smith Act
pro bono
prosecuting attorney
religious test
selective incorporation of the Bill of Rights
slander
subpoena
test case
warrant
zones of privacy
Bail Reform Act
probable cause
procedural due process
public defender
salutary neglect
self-incrimination
shared-time
Solomon Agreement
substantive due process
use immunity
writ of habeas corpus

Civil Rights

at-large election
single-member district election
Brown v. Board of Education of Topeka
civil disobedience
comparable worth
primary election
affirmative action
attentive public
bilingual education

civil rights
de facto segregation
de jure segregation
Dred Scott case
equal opportunity
Equal Rights Amendment (ERA)
gerrymandering
integration
legislative appointment
minority business set-aside
minority-vote packing
NAACP
racially restrictive covenants
reverse discrimination
statutory law
suffrage
test case
test of understanding
title IX
Simpson-Mazzoli Immigration Act
disfranchisement
Emancipation Proclamation
equal protection
equality of result
grandfather clause
Jim Crow laws
literacy test
minority-vote dilution
poll tax
racial quota
restrictive covenant
reasonable basis test
"separate but equal"
strict judicial scrutiny
suspect classification doctrine
white primary
Voting Rights Act of 1965
Civil Rights Act of 1964

SAMPLE OUTLINE

Comparable worth is one of the most controversial issues of the women's and civil rights movements. In this outline, the topic is split into three parts: the background of comparable worth, arguments for comparable worth, and arguments against comparable worth.

THE DEBATE OVER COMPARABLE WORTH

I. **Comparable worth came out of inequities between women's and men's salaries**
   A. Women earned only 60 percent of what men earned in the 1980s
   B. Women constituted 70 percent of the work force in 80 percent of the fields in which they worked
   C. Comparable worth tries to institute the idea of equal pay for equal work
      1. Some professions pay too little simply because women dominate them
      2. Pay should depend on the skill level of the job
   D. Attempts have been made to address comparable worth
      1. Equal Pay Act
      2. AFSCME lawsuit
   E. Comparable worth is not the law of the land
      1. Requires a difficult job evaluation
      2. Some states have adopted comparable worth

II. Arguments for comparable worth

A. The pay gap is narrowing, but at a slow pace; therefore, comparable worth is essential

B. The gap is a result of discrimination

1. Women often start with the same salaries as men, but men get better raises
2. Women are not given the same opportunities for promotion

C. Existing anti-discrimination laws have done little good

D. Market forces are not the solution

1. Employers will give women lower pay, regardless of the woman's qualifications or the demand for her skills
2. States like Minnesota that have comparable worth have only had a modest rise in payroll outlays

E. Government would not have to set pay, just check that pay is equitable

III. Arguments against comparable worth

A. Pay gap between men and women is not so large

1. Only full-time, year-round jobs are counted
2. Jobs like teaching are not counted

B. Flexible jobs often pay less to allow women to have and raise families

C. Existing anti-discrimination laws are enough

D. Market rates should be allowed to prevail

1. Supply and demand insure that any worker is paid his or her true worth
2. Tampering with the free market will impede the strength of U.S. business

E. Comparable worth could be expensive

F. Government might be put in the position of providing wages

G. Comparable worth might discourage women from making inroads into new professions, and thus lock them into traditional women's professions

CHRONOLOGY I

Supreme Court Cases Affecting Civil Liberties

1833 *Barron v. Baltimore* limited the application of the Bill of Rights to cases involving the federal government. Barron appealed to the Supreme Court because he felt that the city of Baltimore violated his Fifth Amendment rights by making his wharf unusable. The Supreme Court rejected his appeal, stating that the original purpose of the Bill of Rights is to stop oppression from the federal level.

1898 *United States v. Wong Kim Ark* allowed for anyone born in the United States to be granted the right of citizenship, even if his/her parents were aliens.

1900 *Maxwell v. Dow* decided that it does not necessarily violate someone's civil rights to have a jury of less than 12 people.

1908 *Twining v. New Jersey* stated that exemption from self-incrimination is not guaranteed to citizens; therefore, states cannot amend that right.

1919 *Schenck v. United States* upheld the Espionage Act of 1917 by sustaining the conviction of a Socialist party officer who had urged young men to dodge the draft.

1925 *Gitlow v. New York* upheld a state statute against advocating the overthrow of the government. The lasting importance of this decision comes from the following statement which brings the Bill of Rights under the protection of the Fourteenth Amendment: "For present purposes we may and do assume that freedom of speech and of the press—which are protected by the First Amendment from abridgment by Congress—are among the fundamental personal rights and 'liberties' protected by the due process clause of the Fourteenth Amendment from impairment by the states."

1925 *Pierce v. Society of Sisters* allowed students in Oregon to attend accredited parochial and private schools before the eighth grade.

1927 *Whitney v. California* upheld the California Criminal Syndicalism Act of 1919 by sustaining the conviction of Anita Whitney, a member of the Communist Labor Party of California, on the grounds that the party advocated violence and terrorism.

1928 *Olmstead v. United States* rules that it was not a violation of unreasonable searches and seizures when federal agents entered certain premises without permission and set up wiretaps.

1930 *Patton v. United States* ruled that it was permissible for a jury to have made a decision with eleven jurors after one of them became ill.

1931 *Stromberg v. California* struck down California's "anti-red-flag" law, arguing that the peaceful display of a red flag, regardless of its symbolic meaning, is a right protected by the First Amendment.

1937 *De Jonge v. Oregon* broadened Fourteenth Amendment protection to include peaceable assembly.

1937 *Palko v. Connecticut* maintained that a state could appeal a criminal case to a higher court and not have it be considered double jeopardy (and thus unconstitutional).

1938 *Johnson v. Zerbst* reversed a conviction of a defendant whose grounds for defense were that he was not familiar enough with the law, and therefore, did not receive the proper rights to counsel.

1940 *Thornhill v. Alabama* upheld a citizen's right to peacefully picket by declaring a state law against "loitering or picketing" unconstitutional.

1940 *Cantwell v. Connecticut* declared for the first time that the Fourteenth Amendment's due process clause applies to states in terms of protection of First Amendment guarantees.

1940 *Chambers v. Florida* ruled that due process was denied when confessions were obtained from four African Americans after submitting them to extreme duress.

1940, 1943 **Flag-Salute Cases**: *Minersville School District v. Gobitas* agreed that students should be required to say the pledge of allegiance, regardless of religious or other objections. *West Virginia State Board of Education v. Barnette* reversed this decision on the grounds that it violates the Fourteenth Amendment.

1942 *Chaplinsky v. New Hampshire* supported certain limits to the right to free speech when it came to lewd, obscene, libelous, or profane expressions or words.

1948 *McCollum v. Board of Education* held that when an Illinois school allowed representatives from the Catholic, Jewish, and Protestant faiths to give religious instruction during school hours, it had violated the constitutional separation of church and state.

1950 *American Communications Association v. Douds* upheld the provision of the Taft-Hartley Labor Management Relations Act of 1947, which had denied certain privileges to unions that did not force their officials to take noncommunist loyalty oaths.

1951 *Dennis v. United States* supported the Smith Act's outlawing of those who willfully advocate the overthrow of the U.S. government and upheld the convictions of eleven leaders of the American Communist Party.

1952 *Adler v. Board of Education* prohibited a person who advocates the overthrow of the government by violence from being employed within the public school system. This decision sustained New York State's Feinberg law.

1952 *Burstyn v. Wilson* ruled that a state cannot deny a license to show a motion picture because the film is deemed to be sacrilegious.

1952 *Zorach v. Clauson* interpreted the First Amendment establishment clause a bit less narrowly than *Burstyn v. Wilson* when it allowed students to seek religious instruction at a location other than a public school during school hours.

1956 *Ullmann v. United States* upheld the constitutionality of a 1954 act of Congress that had granted immunity from criminal prosecution to those whose testimony was needed for national security.

1957 *Mallory v. United States* invalidated a confession as evidence because the accused had been held for an inordinately long time.

1957 *Yates v. United States* held that a person cannot be convicted simply for advocating a revolutionary philosophy like Marxism.

1957 *Roth v. United States* overturned a decision that had judged a publication that was said to cause impure thoughts as obscene.

1961 *Scales v. United States* reaffirmed the Smith Act.

1961 *Communist Party of America v. Subversive Activities Control Board* forced the American Communist Party to register with the Justice Department in accordance with the Security Act of 1950.

1961 *Mapp v. Ohio* held that if evidence is obtained without an authentic search warrant, it will not be permissible for state or federal prosecution.

1962 *Engel v. Vitale* banned the Regent's Prayer in public schools.

1963 *School District of Abington Township v. Schempp* held that reciting the Lord's Prayer or mandatory reading from the Bible in public school violates the First Amendment.

1964 *Malloy v. Hogan* overruled *Twining v. New Jersey* and *Adamson v. California.*

1965 *Cox v. Louisiana* reversed a state court decision which had convicted a civil rights demonstrator who had blocked the street. The Supreme Court argued that Louisiana had not convicted others in similar demonstrations for different causes, so this conviction was unfair.

1965 *Albertson v. Subversive Activities Control Board* voided provisions in the Internal Security Act and other laws which required communist individuals to register.

1966 *A Book named "John Cleland's Memoirs of a Woman of Pleasure (Fanny Hill)" v. Attorney General of Massachusetts* reversed a state court's decision to ban a book because it was considered prurient and offensive.

1966 *Miranda v. Arizona* held that a suspect held by the police must be fully informed of his/her rights before any questioning. This protection is based on the Fourth and Fifteenth Amendments.

1967 *Keyishan v. Board of Regents* overruled *Adler v. Board of Education.*

1968 *Katz v. United States* reversed *Olmstead v. United States*; it brought electronic surveillance equipment, such as wiretaps, under the purview of the Fourteenth Amendment's prohibition against unreasonable searches and seizures.

1968 *Board of Education v. Allen* approved the lending of secular school books to parochial schools in New York State.

1968 *United States v. O'Brien* supported the incidental limitation of First Amendment freedoms only if the government does so for the greater good (such as waging war), but not for the suppression of freedom. The conviction of a young man who burned his draft card was sustained.

1969 *Benton v. Maryland* strengthened a citizen's protection from double jeopardy by overruling *Paldo v. Connecticut.*

1970 *Walz v. Tax Commission of the City of New York* affirmed the tax-exempt status for churches and land used for religious purposes.

1971 *Lemon v. Kurtzman* declared Pennsylvania and Rhode Island laws which gave funds to religious schools unconstitutional. The court decided that these two states were in violation of the First and Fourteenth Amendments.

1971 *Tilton v. Richardson* upheld a 1963 Act of Congress which had allowed the federal government to give aid for the construction of buildings on private- or church-related colleges.

1972 *United States v. United States District Court for the Eastern District of Michigan* declared a common practice of wiretapping those suspected of domestic subversion unconstitutional.

1972 *Furman v. Georgia* ruled that since the death penalty was used so infrequently, it should be considered cruel and unusual punishment, and therefore violates the Eighth and Fourteenth Amendments.

1973 *Miller v. California* rejected the previous test for judging whether something was obscene, and stated that a community could use its own standards to judge obscenity.

1974 *Communist Party of Indiana v. Whitcomb* invalidated a state law that had banned from the ballot candidates who had not taken an oath not to overthrow the government by force.

1974 *United States v. Matlock* made an exception to the unreasonable-search-and-seizure clause by allowing evidence to be used in court if a third party (not the accused) gives permission to search a place that he/she has equal authority over.

1975 *O'Connor v. Donaldson* improved the rights of mental patients by holding that their right to liberty was injured if they were held against their will, or held after it was proven that they could take care of themselves and are not dangerous to others.

1975 *Taylor v. Louisiana* reversed a rape conviction because state laws had excluded women from the jury pool.

1976 *Proffitt v. Florida* ruled that the death penalty was not in violation of the Eighth or Fourteenth Amendment.

1977 *Wooley v. Maynard* declared a New Hampshire law requiring passenger automobiles to have the state motto, "Live Free or Die," on their license plates unconstitutional.

CHRONOLOGY II

Supreme Court Cases Affecting Civil Rights

1857 *Dred Scott v. Sandford* denied a slave his freedom, even though he had lived in a territory where slavery was outlawed, on the grounds that he was not a citizen and thus did not have the rights of a citizen.

1880 *Strauder v. West Virginia* declared unconstitutional a West Virginia statute which required that all jurors be white.

1883 Civil Rights Cases void the Civil Rights Act of 1875, which had given states the right to set up whatever racial restrictions they desired.

1896 *Plessy v. Ferguson* affirmed the concept of "separate but equal" as an acceptable standard for treatment of minorities.

1915 *Truax v. Raich* struck down a state law that had required employers to hire U.S. citizens as 80 percent of their work force.

1917 *Buchanan v. Warley* voided a city ordinance which had required the separation of blacks and whites.

1932 *Powell v. Alabama* (First Scottsboro Case) reversed an African American's conviction for rape on the grounds that the trial had not provided an adequate defense council.

1935 *Norris v. Alabama* (Second Scottsboro Case) reversed a conviction of an African American on rape charges because of the long-term practice of excluding African Americans from the jury.

1938 *Missouri ex rel. Gaines v. Canada* modified the "separate but equal" doctrine by declaring that if a comparable school for African Americans is not available, then African Americans should be allowed to attend white schools.

1950 *McLaurin v. Oklahoma State Regents* declared that denying a graduate student at the University of Oklahoma access to white cafeterias, classrooms, libraries, etc., violated his Fourteenth Amendment guarantee to equal protection.

1950 *Sweat v. Painter* ordered that an African American student be admitted to a white law school in Texas, even though one for African Americans existed, on the grounds that the separate schools were not equal.

1955, 1956 *Brown v. Board of Education of Topeka* struck down the "separate but equal" precedent established by *Plessy v. Ferguson*.

1968 *Jones v. Alfred H. Mayer Co.* revived an 1866 act of Congress, saying that there could be no racial discrimination in the sale or rental of property.

1971 *Swann v. Charlotte-Mecklenburg County Board of Education* decided that desegregation does not necessarily mean that each school's student population must reflect the racial composition of the surrounding school district.

1973 *Roe v. Wade* legalized abortion in all states.

1974 *Cleveland Board of Education v. Le Fleur* discarded a regulation that had set requirements for when a pregnant teacher must take leave without pay and for when she can return to the job.

1974 *Milliken v. Bradley* rejected a busing plan for the Detroit public school system on the grounds that no racial segregation was shown to have happened.

1976 *Washington v. Davis* agreed that a racially neutral hiring policy cannot be considered discriminatory.

1976 *Planned Parenthood of Central Missouri v. Danforth* increased abortion rights for women by declaring a Missouri law requiring children under 18 years of age to get their parents' permission before they obtain an abortion unconstitutional.

1977 *Beal v. Doe* gave states broad discretionary powers as to how much financial support they would provide for nontherapeutic abortions.

1977 *Califano v. Goldfarb* helped the cause of "men's liberation" by deciding that, just as widows are entitled to their deceased husband's Social Security benefits, so should widowers be equally entitled.

1978 *Regents of the University of California v. Bakke* decided that quotas for accepting minority students were not permissible under the Civil Rights Act of 1964.

SHORT READING LIST

Irving Brant, *The Bill of Rights*. Gives a solid treatment of the origins of civil liberties guaranteed by the Constitution.

Richard C. Cortner, *The Supreme Court and the Second Bill of Rights*. Provides a comprehensive account of how the Bill of Rights was interpreted and incorporated into common use by Supreme Court decisions.

Leonard W. Levy, *Emergence of a Free Press*. Reviews the development of free speech from early to relatively recent times.

Robert Cord, *Separation of Church and State*. Covers the issue of separation of church and state.

Richard Kluger, *Simple Justice*. Deals with the efforts made to achieve racial equality.

Charles S. Bullock III and Charles M. Lamb, *Implementation of Civil Rights Policy*. Covers all types of civil rights issues in a concise manner.

Ethel Klein, *Gender Politics*. Explores political questions concerning women.

Henry Abraham, *Freedom and the Court: Civil Rights and Liberties in the United States*, 5th ed. Provides a historical survey of the growth and development of civil liberties and civil rights.

John Brigham, *Civil Liberties and American Democracy*. Analyzes different opinions of civil rights and civil liberties.

Eleanor Flexner, *Century of Struggle: The Women's Rights Movement in the United States*. Covers the women's rights movement from the nineteenth century to the present.

PART 3

Practice Tests

PRACTICE TEST 1

PRACTICE TEST 2

PRACTICE TEST 1

Answer Sheet

1. Ⓐ Ⓑ Ⓒ Ⓓ Ⓔ	13. Ⓐ Ⓑ Ⓒ Ⓓ Ⓔ	25. Ⓐ Ⓑ Ⓒ Ⓓ Ⓔ	37. Ⓐ Ⓑ Ⓒ Ⓓ Ⓔ	49. Ⓐ Ⓑ Ⓒ Ⓓ Ⓔ
2. Ⓐ Ⓑ Ⓒ Ⓓ Ⓔ	14. Ⓐ Ⓑ Ⓒ Ⓓ Ⓔ	26. Ⓐ Ⓑ Ⓒ Ⓓ Ⓔ	38. Ⓐ Ⓑ Ⓒ Ⓓ Ⓔ	50. Ⓐ Ⓑ Ⓒ Ⓓ Ⓔ
3. Ⓐ Ⓑ Ⓒ Ⓓ Ⓔ	15. Ⓐ Ⓑ Ⓒ Ⓓ Ⓔ	27. Ⓐ Ⓑ Ⓒ Ⓓ Ⓔ	39. Ⓐ Ⓑ Ⓒ Ⓓ Ⓔ	51. Ⓐ Ⓑ Ⓒ Ⓓ Ⓔ
4. Ⓐ Ⓑ Ⓒ Ⓓ Ⓔ	16. Ⓐ Ⓑ Ⓒ Ⓓ Ⓔ	28. Ⓐ Ⓑ Ⓒ Ⓓ Ⓔ	40. Ⓐ Ⓑ Ⓒ Ⓓ Ⓔ	52. Ⓐ Ⓑ Ⓒ Ⓓ Ⓔ
5. Ⓐ Ⓑ Ⓒ Ⓓ Ⓔ	17. Ⓐ Ⓑ Ⓒ Ⓓ Ⓔ	29. Ⓐ Ⓑ Ⓒ Ⓓ Ⓔ	41. Ⓐ Ⓑ Ⓒ Ⓓ Ⓔ	53. Ⓐ Ⓑ Ⓒ Ⓓ Ⓔ
6. Ⓐ Ⓑ Ⓒ Ⓓ Ⓔ	18. Ⓐ Ⓑ Ⓒ Ⓓ Ⓔ	30. Ⓐ Ⓑ Ⓒ Ⓓ Ⓔ	42. Ⓐ Ⓑ Ⓒ Ⓓ Ⓔ	54. Ⓐ Ⓑ Ⓒ Ⓓ Ⓔ
7. Ⓐ Ⓑ Ⓒ Ⓓ Ⓔ	19. Ⓐ Ⓑ Ⓒ Ⓓ Ⓔ	31. Ⓐ Ⓑ Ⓒ Ⓓ Ⓔ	43. Ⓐ Ⓑ Ⓒ Ⓓ Ⓔ	55. Ⓐ Ⓑ Ⓒ Ⓓ Ⓔ
8. Ⓐ Ⓑ Ⓒ Ⓓ Ⓔ	20. Ⓐ Ⓑ Ⓒ Ⓓ Ⓔ	32. Ⓐ Ⓑ Ⓒ Ⓓ Ⓔ	44. Ⓐ Ⓑ Ⓒ Ⓓ Ⓔ	56. Ⓐ Ⓑ Ⓒ Ⓓ Ⓔ
9. Ⓐ Ⓑ Ⓒ Ⓓ Ⓔ	21. Ⓐ Ⓑ Ⓒ Ⓓ Ⓔ	33. Ⓐ Ⓑ Ⓒ Ⓓ Ⓔ	45. Ⓐ Ⓑ Ⓒ Ⓓ Ⓔ	57. Ⓐ Ⓑ Ⓒ Ⓓ Ⓔ
10. Ⓐ Ⓑ Ⓒ Ⓓ Ⓔ	22. Ⓐ Ⓑ Ⓒ Ⓓ Ⓔ	34. Ⓐ Ⓑ Ⓒ Ⓓ Ⓔ	46. Ⓐ Ⓑ Ⓒ Ⓓ Ⓔ	58. Ⓐ Ⓑ Ⓒ Ⓓ Ⓔ
11. Ⓐ Ⓑ Ⓒ Ⓓ Ⓔ	23. Ⓐ Ⓑ Ⓒ Ⓓ Ⓔ	35. Ⓐ Ⓑ Ⓒ Ⓓ Ⓔ	47. Ⓐ Ⓑ Ⓒ Ⓓ Ⓔ	59. Ⓐ Ⓑ Ⓒ Ⓓ Ⓔ
12. Ⓐ Ⓑ Ⓒ Ⓓ Ⓔ	24. Ⓐ Ⓑ Ⓒ Ⓓ Ⓔ	36. Ⓐ Ⓑ Ⓒ Ⓓ Ⓔ	48. Ⓐ Ⓑ Ⓒ Ⓓ Ⓔ	60. Ⓐ Ⓑ Ⓒ Ⓓ Ⓔ

GO ON TO THE NEXT PAGE

Practice Test 1

UNITED STATES GOVERNMENT AND POLITICS

Multiple Choice

Time—45 Minutes

60 Questions

Directions: *Each of the questions or incomplete statements below is followed by five possible answer choices. Select the one choice that best answers the question or completes the statement and fill in the corresponding oval on the answer sheet.*

1. Which of the following courts is NOT part of the federal judicial system?
   (A) The Washington, D.C. Municipal Court
   (B) The Territorial Court of the Virgin Islands
   (C) The U.S. District Courts
   (D) The Police Court of New York City
   (E) The Court of Military Appeals

2. Federal and state governments of the U.S. share the power to
   (A) establish schools
   (B) conduct foreign relations
   (C) establish post offices
   (D) charter banks
   (E) issue money

3. What is the proper chronology for the following documents:
   I. Petition of Right
   II. Bill of Rights
   III. Declaration of Independence
   IV. Magna Carta
   (A) I, II, III, IV
   (B) II, I, III, IV
   (C) III, I, II, IV
   (D) IV, I, III, II
   (E) I, IV, III, II

4. The following statement can be found in which part of the Constitution? "All persons born or naturalized in the United States, and subject to the jurisdiction thereof, are citizens of the United States and of the State wherein they reside. No State shall make or enforce any law which shall abridge the privileges or immunities of citizens of the United States; nor shall any State deprive any person of life, liberty, or property, without due process of law; nor deny to any person within its jurisdiction the equal protection of the laws."
   (A) Fourteenth Amendment
   (B) Preamble
   (C) Article One, Section 5
   (D) Article One, Section 10
   (E) Bill of Rights

5. "No person held to service or labour in one State, under the laws thereof, escaping into another shall, in consequence of any law or regulation therein, be discharged from such service or labour, but shall be delivered up on claim of the party to whom such service or labour may be due." This statement from Article Four of the U.S. Constitution can best be described as
   (A) an example of the ability of the Constitution to be adapted to the changing needs of the country
   (B) an example of how state governments have the power to regulate commerce between states
   (C) an example of how the Constitution did not always uphold the ideals of equality for all men
   (D) an example of how the Constitution has consistently upheld civil rights
   (E) an example of the changes to the Constitution after the Civil War

GO ON TO THE NEXT PAGE

6. What principle protects citizens from being punished twice for the same crime?
   (A) trial by jury
   (B) presentment
   (C) double jeopardy
   (D) self-incrimination
   (E) due process

7. What is the best example of close interaction between the two houses of the legislature?
   (A) iron triangle
   (B) joint committees
   (C) standing committees
   (D) dual branch committees
   (E) select committees

8. Political action committees are sometimes criticized for
   (A) limiting themselves to being only grass-roots organizations
   (B) being dominated by foreign interests
   (C) never supporting incumbent candidates
   (D) encouraging strict campaign finance regulations
   (E) making politicians dependent on their financial support

9. All the following are true about the majority leader of the Senate EXCEPT
   (A) He or she is the leader of the Senate majority party.
   (B) He or she is recognized first in debate.
   (C) He or she controls the scheduling of bills for floor consideration.
   (D) He or she has more power than Senate whips.
   (E) He or she is always selected from a different party than the vice president.

10. *Marbury v. Madison* is considered a critical Supreme Court case because it established the precedent of
   (A) judicial review
   (B) appellate jurisdiction
   (C) juris prudence
   (D) original jurisdiction
   (E) checks and balances

11. The law that did the most to speed the demise of the spoils system and made merit the key qualification for hiring government civil servants was
   (A) the Civil Service Reform Act of 1978
   (B) the Pendleton Act of 1883
   (C) the Hatch Act of 1939
   (D) the Garfield Amendment of 1902
   (E) the Civil Service Reform Act of 1946

12. The most effective way that the Federal Reserve System can be used by the government to influence the economy is to
   (A) close banks which lend excessively to foreign countries and seldom to U.S. citizens
   (B) take large amounts of money out of circulation in order to curb inflation
   (C) raise or lower interests in order to influence interest rates of private banks
   (D) levy taxes on luxury items in order to create more revenue for the government
   (E) create new business by selling parts of federal agencies to the private sector

13. All the following have been suggested by experts as reasons for low voter turnout in the United States EXCEPT
   (A) literacy requirements for voters
   (B) cumbersome registration requirements
   (C) weakening power of political parties
   (D) apathy on the part of the electorate
   (E) disillusionment with politics in general

14. The Smith Act of 1940 occasionally put labor unions and the federal government at odds with each other because
   (A) many labor unions were suspected of having communists or socialists among their membership who might advocate the violent overthrow of the government
   (B) the Smith Act forbade practices that might impede the profitable functioning of a business
   (C) the Smith Act forbade strikes in areas that were crucial to the functioning of the economy
   (D) wages set by the Smith Act were often lower than the wages which many workers were currently receiving

(E) many labor union members expected consultation by the staff members of legislators before they made a law which would so profoundly affect union membership

15. What is most accurate statement about political participation and political parties?
    (A) Voters feel a stronger affiliation to their political parties when they are voting for president than when voting for a congressional representative.
    (B) The Democratic and Republican parties hold conventions to nominate their presidential candidates in order to discourage participation by low-ranking members.
    (C) In major elections, there is usually a third major party that emerges to challenge the Republicans and Democrats.
    (D) The stronger the grass-roots support for a party, the more divisive the nominating conventions are likely to be.
    (E) The trend over the last 50 years has been a lessening of party loyalty, especially in national elections.

Party Identification and Economic Status

Party	Income Status Relative to the National Average		
	Bottom 1/3	Middle 1/3	Top 1/3
Democratic	34%	35%	31%
Republican	22%	34%	44%
Independent	33%	34%	33%
Undeclared	49%	31%	20%

16. According to the information provided above, which of the following statements is most accurate?
    (A) There were more undeclared candidates than Democratic candidates.
    (B) Republican membership contains a majority of people in the top 1/3 in income status.
    (C) Republicans and Democrats have an equal number of people in the middle 1/3 in income status.
    (D) Republicans and Independents have an equal proportion of their members in the middle income status.
    (E) Democrats, Republicans, Independents, and Undeclareds have an equal number of members.

17. Suppose that 30 percent of registered Republican voters who opposed the Republican platform on abortion rights voted for a different candidate as a protest vote, and at the same time 39 percent of the registered Democrats voted Republican because of their strong support for the Republican platform on abortion rights.

    Which of the following hypotheses is LEAST supportable by this information?
    (A) Many voters are single-issue voters.
    (B) Party affiliation is no longer a strong influence on voting patterns.
    (C) Party platforms are formed with the purpose of bringing in a diverse group of supporters.
    (D) The amount of voters gained and lost by the abortion stance almost equalled out.
    (E) Abortion is a key issue for a candidate.

18. Republicans referring to previous epochs in their party's history that could be used to persuade minority groups to join would have the most success using which of the following examples?
    (A) Herbert Hoover's economic policies
    (B) Richard Nixon's treatment of college student protesters
    (C) Abraham Lincoln's election platform
    (D) Teddy Roosevelt's African safaris
    (E) George Bush's stance on Haitian refugees

19. "Grandfather clauses" in the late nineteenth and early twentieth centuries, which required all prospective voters either to pay a tax or pass a test except for those whose grandfathers had been eligible to vote, had the effect of
    (A) keeping the children of illiterates from voting
    (B) weeding out people who would not vote wisely
    (C) preventing women from voting
    (D) discriminating against the elderly
    (E) keeping African-Americans from voting

GO ON TO THE NEXT PAGE

Questions 20–21 refer to the following excerpt from a United States Supreme Court decision:

"For present purposes we may and do assume that freedom of speech and of press—which are protected from abridgement by Congress—are among the fundamental personal rights and liberties protected by the due process clause of the Fourteenth Amendment from impairment by the states."

20. This decision by the Supreme Court was important because
    (A) it strengthened the power of states to interpret the Constitution
    (B) it affirmed the power of the Supreme Court to have the final say in interpreting the Bill of Rights
    (C) it led to the eventual overturning of the Fourteenth Amendment
    (D) it placed more stringent limits on freedom of speech
    (E) it weakened federalism in favor of a system that more equitably balanced state versus federal powers

21. This decision would most likely have significance for
    (A) a person accused of sedition by Congress
    (B) a person found guilty of slander against a mayor and jailed by local authorities
    (C) a union organizer accused of murder
    (D) a Senator accused of perjury by a political opponent
    (E) a doctor being sued for malpractice in two different states

22. If legislation stalls before it reaches the House floor for debate, it can most likely be found in which committee?
    (A) Ethics Committee
    (B) Committee on Committees
    (C) Foreign Relations Committee
    (D) Ways and Means Committee
    (E) Rules Committee

23. Impoundments are most likely to be used by the president to
    (A) release prisoners he feels were falsely incarcerated
    (B) take property from people who did not pay taxes
    (C) control illegal narcotics imports
    (D) strip errant legislators of their powers
    (E) control Congress's spending through the refusal to use funds

24. A president has the most unchecked authority when he or she is
    (A) creating and implementing the national budget
    (B) negotiating and signing treaties with foreign nations
    (C) creating and passing legislation
    (D) repelling sudden attacks on the U.S.
    (E) formally declaring war

25. Which of the following statements supports the elitist theory of U.S. politics?
    (A) To be elected, politicians must earn the support of a large cross section of the electorate.
    (B) Political action committees often support candidates of meager financial means.
    (C) In the last two decades, almost every mainstream candidate for the presidency has been a millionaire.
    (D) Business leaders are often in disagreement over policy and political candidates.
    (E) There are more registered Democrats than Republicans.

26. Which of the following theories about the president's political approval rating and military action is best supported by historical examples?
    (A) The longer and more protracted a war is, the higher and stronger the current president's approval rating will be.
    (B) Short successful military engagements are followed by a sharp rise in the president's approval rating.
    (C) Every president tries to have at least one military action during his/her presidency, in order to solidify public approval.
    (D) Presidents are always blamed when wars are lost and lauded when wars are won.
    (E) The higher the casualty rate of the enemy during a war, the higher the president's approval rating will be.

27. One factor which would support the practice of keeping federal bureaucrats in office longer than politicians is that
    (A) the government depends on bureaucrats' expertise in different areas that makes them hard to replace
    (B) bureaucrats leaving office often blow the whistle on wasteful government practices
    (C) government agencies are required by law to be free of political considerations
    (D) it is hard to fill agency positions since the hours are long and the pay is low
    (E) it will prevent assassinations like President Garfield's

28. One of the best ways that the federal Department of Education has to influence national education policy is
    (A) establishing new schools where they are needed
    (B) setting conditions for the distribution of financial aid
    (C) hiring and firing teachers
    (D) dictating standards to be used in certifying teachers
    (E) closing schools that do not meet basic federal standards

29. Which person would most likely be paid a high salary to lobby for a large defense contractor?
    (A) an unemployed factory worker who needs part-time work while he goes back to school
    (B) an ex-government official who had a high position in the defense department
    (C) an antiwar protestor who has often lobbied in Washington
    (D) an enlisted soldier stationed near Washington, D.C.
    (E) a high-level official in the current administration

30. Which of the following would most likely be criticized by those who feel that the presidential election process is not democratic enough?
    (A) the electoral college
    (B) media coverage
    (C) state primaries
    (D) presidential debates
    (E) third-party candidates

31. The popularity of media consultants in political campaigns points to
    (A) the increasing importance of door-to-door campaigning
    (B) the decreasing size of campaign budgets
    (C) the waning popularity of daily newspapers
    (D) the increasing need for candidates to be well-versed in the technical aspects of TV camera work
    (E) the importance of creating the desired television image and being able to create a negative television image for the opponent

32. All of the following are common steps to the passage of a bill by Congress EXCEPT
    (A) introduction into both the Senate and the House
    (B) referral to committees for recommendations
    (C) presidential approval of committee recommendations
    (D) House and Senate debate
    (E) House and Senate compromise

33. A judicial restraintist is most likely to
    (A) apply judicial review whenever possible
    (B) place the wishes of elected representatives as a high priority
    (C) apply liberal philosophy to Supreme Court decisions
    (D) hear large numbers of cases
    (E) block many executive initiatives

GO ON TO THE NEXT PAGE

34. The Treasury Note pictured above would most likely be issued by the federal government to
    (A) pay back a foreign loan
    (B) give an alternative to the cash tax refund
    (C) raise money for a war in progress
    (D) finance budget deficits
    (E) increase the circulation of hard currency

35. Which of the following amendments to the Constitution had a large impact on U.S. voting practices?
    I. Fifteenth Amendment
    II. Nineteenth Amendment
    III. Twentieth Amendment
    IV. Twenty-sixth Amendment
    (A) I only
    (B) I and II
    (C) I, II, and III
    (D) II, III, and IV
    (E) I, II, IV

36. What would be one likely reason for a president to enter into an executive agreement with a foreign country rather than sign a treaty?
    (A) An executive agreement avoids political wrangling with the Senate since it does not need to be ratified.
    (B) An executive agreement has more legal validity than a treaty.
    (C) A president can easily back down from an executive agreement with no recourse for the foreign country.
    (D) The Case Act of 1972 encouraged executive agreements.
    (E) An executive agreement requires prior Senate approval, making resulting negotiations easier for the president.

37. The Environmental Protection Agency (EPA) could most likely be expected to run into resistance to its policies from
    (A) environmentalists who feel that policies go too far and sacrifice the economy because of environmental concerns
    (B) farmers who want more protection for their livestock
    (C) business interests that resent the high cost of environmental protection measures
    (D) doctors who have fewer patients as the environment becomes cleaner
    (E) universities that resent having to do environmental research for the government

38. Which of the following is the most accurate statement about presidential veto power?
    (A) Vetoes are used on over 50 percent of the bills that pass through the White House.
    (B) Republicans have been more likely to veto bills than have Democrats.
    (C) It is the most effective way for a president to influence the legislative process.
    (D) A veto is final and Congress has no method of undoing it.
    (E) The use of the veto has declined in the last 30 years.

THE "BRAINS"

39. This cartoon depiction of a nineteenth-century politician is most likely trying to make which of the following commentaries?
    (A) Money is essential to winning a campaign.
    (B) Most politicians are overweight.
    (C) Money can take the place of other important considerations for a politician.
    (D) A successful politician will enable his supporters to earn large amounts of money.
    (E) Wealthy politicians often are the most intelligent.

40. Which of the following agencies would be the most useful to a congressional member concerned about the safety of a nuclear power plant?
    (A) the Congressional Research Service
    (B) the General Accounting Office
    (C) the Office of Automation
    (D) the Congressional Budget Office
    (E) the Office of Technology Assessment

41. The Gulf of Tonkin Resolution was significant because
    (A) it limited the president's power to use military force
    (B) it was a result of the War Powers Resolution
    (C) it gave the president more flexibility regarding when and how to use military force
    (D) it showed how Congress was opposed to giving more power to the president
    (E) it led to the end of the Vietnam War

42. The U.S. government since the Great Depression can be fairly described as all of the following EXCEPT
    (A) smaller and less involved in people's daily welfare
    (B) having more services for the needy
    (C) more socialistic in terms of public assistance of programs
    (D) having larger budgets and more expenses
    (E) having more control over people's lives than many of the founders of the Constitution envisioned

43. All of the following can be considered important to the effectiveness of a lobbyist EXCEPT
    (A) demonstrable grass-roots support for his/her stand on an issue
    (B) connections with important decision makers
    (C) large financial resources to spend on politicians
    (D) familiarity with the political process
    (E) good communications ability

GO ON TO THE NEXT PAGE

Questions 44–45 are based on the following Supreme Court decision:

"Although the Court has not assumed to define 'liberty' with any great precision, that term is not confined to mere freedom from bodily restraint. Liberty under law extends to the full range of conduct which the individual is free to pursue, and it cannot be restricted except for a proper governmental objective.

Segregation in public education is not reasonably related to any proper governmental objective, and thus it imposes on Negro children of the District of Columbia a burden that constitutes an arbitrary deprivation of their liberty in violation of the Due Process Clause.

In view of our decision that the Constitution prohibits the states from maintaining racially segregated public schools, it would be unthinkable that the same Constitution would impose a lesser duty on the Federal Government. We hold that racial segregation in the public schools of the District of Columbia is a denial of the Due Process of law guaranteed by the Fifth Amendment of the Constitution."

44. The opinions expressed in this decision are closest to those of
    (A) *Plessy v. Ferguson*
    (B) *McCulloch v. Maryland*
    (C) *Brown v. Board of Education of Topeka*
    (D) *Zorach v. Clauson*
    (E) *Near v. Minnesota*

45. Which statement about liberty is the Supreme Court justices who wrote this decision likely to agree with?
    (A) States should decide what the definition of liberty is.
    (B) The definition of liberty is clearly set out in the Constitution.
    (C) Liberty must be redefined with every Court decision.
    (D) Segregation denies black people their liberty.
    (E) Liberty simply means freedom from being physically enslaved.

46. Which of the following was an argument in favor of federalism prior to the ratification of the Constitution.
    (A) The corrupt state governments would lose power.
    (B) Federalism had already worked in several other countries.
    (C) States would hold the majority of governmental power.
    (D) A unified group of states could better protect the people.
    (E) Having several levels of government would be unwieldy.

47. All of the following were in the Articles of Confederation and were later changed in the Constitution EXCEPT
    (A) provision for Canada to join the United States
    (B) states pay national expenses to Congress
    (C) state legislatures appoint all militia under the rank of colonel
    (D) state legislatures select delegates to Congress
    (E) sole power to make peace and war is given to Congress

48. Which of the following cabinet departments has had the highest budget and number of employees?
    (A) Department of Defense
    (B) Department of Education
    (C) Department of Agriculture
    (D) Department of Energy
    (E) Department of State

49. The majority leader of the Senate would most likely wish to serve on which of the following committees and at what capacity?
    (A) chair of a Select Committee on Ethics
    (B) chair of the Joint Library Committee
    (C) senior member of the Rules Committee
    (D) chair of the Appropriations Committee
    (E) minority chair of the Foreign Relations Committee

50. Which of the following positions on the government payroll is most likely to have job security free from the vagaries of politics and elections?
    (A) a Senator's legislative assistant
    (B) a commissioner of an independent regulatory agency
    (C) a House member's case worker
    (D) the secretary of state
    (E) the president's press secretary

51. Which of the following is NOT an important milestone in U.S. liberalism?
    (A) Civil Rights Act of 1964
    (B) deregulation of many industries in the 1980s
    (C) the New Deal reforms of the 1930s
    (D) Lyndon Johnson's Great Society
    (E) the Populist party convention of 1892

52. All of the following factors add to public disillusionment with members of Congress in terms of their integrity and effectiveness EXCEPT
    (A) pork-barrel politics
    (B) logrolling
    (C) Abscam of 1980
    (D) frequent use of franking privileges
    (E) the hours currently spent on the job as compared to 100 years ago

53. Which statement about the Supreme Court and economic policy is most accurate?
    (A) Historically, the Supreme Court has had little influence on the economy.
    (B) Judicial restraintists believe that the Court has a responsibility to influence economic policy.
    (C) There has been a clear increase in the extent to which the Supreme Court has involved itself in the economy.
    (D) In the decades after the Civil War, the Supreme Court played a major role in economic policy.
    (E) Most historians have applauded the role that the Supreme Court played during and after the Great Depression.

54. Which factor was the LEAST important in influencing voter tendencies in the 1992 presidential campaign?
    (A) prolonged economic recession
    (B) wide-ranged dissatisfaction with "politics as usual"
    (C) foreign crisis in Asia
    (D) presidential debates
    (E) perceived integrity of the candidates

55. Which of the following factors are most important to determining a group's effectiveness in terms of the extent to which it influences politics?
    I. size
    II. closeness to societal consensus
    III. racial composition
    IV. organizational effectiveness
    (A) I only
    (B) I, IV only
    (C) I, II, III, IV
    (D) I, II, IV
    (E) III, IV

56. All of the following were important elements in the framing of the Constitution EXCEPT
    (A) the Kentucky and Virginia Resolutions
    (B) the New Jersey Plan
    (C) the Great Compromise
    (D) the three-fifths compromise
    (E) the Virginia Plan

57. Opponents to the concept of comparable worth advocated by NOW and other women's rights groups would most likely argue that
    (A) women have always had the same rights as men
    (B) it would increase expenses and make U.S. business less competitive
    (C) women already earn as much as men
    (D) women are physically unable to do many of the higher paying jobs
    (E) it would take away from needed government involvement in business

GO ON TO THE NEXT PAGE

58. How would HUD, under its policies of the last two decades, handle a complaint about unfair housing practices?
    (A) take the accused party to court
    (B) refer the case to Congress for action
    (C) refer the case to the local authorities when possible
    (D) investigate and then fine the accused parties
    (E) fine the state where the infraction took place

59. Minority interest groups would most likely support the Simpson-Mazzoli Immigration Act of 1986 because
    (A) it was designed to encourage illegal immigration
    (B) it favored Hispanic immigrants
    (C) it forced minority immigrants to leave
    (D) it gave many illegal aliens, who were minorities, a chance for citizenship
    (E) it finally opened the U.S./Mexican border

60. Arranging legislative districts to favor incumbent legislators is called
    (A) pork barrel
    (B) apportionment
    (C) ballot stuffing
    (D) affirmative action
    (E) gerrymandering

STOP

THIS IS THE END OF THIS SECTION. YOU MAY CHECK YOUR ANSWERS IN THIS SECTION IF THERE IS EXTRA TIME REMAINING.

Practice Test 1

Quick-Score Answer Key

1.	A	21.	B	41.	C
2.	D	22.	E	42.	A
3.	D	23.	E	43.	C
4.	A	24.	D	44.	C
5.	C	25.	C	45.	D
6.	C	26.	B	46.	D
7.	B	27.	A	47.	E
8.	E	28.	B	48.	A
9.	E	29.	B	49.	D
10.	A	30.	A	50.	B
11.	B	31.	E	51.	B
12.	C	32.	C	52.	E
13.	A	33.	B	53.	D
14.	A	34.	D	54.	C
15.	E	35.	E	55.	D
16.	D	36.	A	56.	A
17.	C	37.	C	57.	B
18.	C	38.	C	58.	C
19.	E	39.	C	59.	D
20.	B	40.	E	60.	E

PRACTICE TEST 1—EXPLANATORY ANSWERS

1. **The correct answer is (A).** As the title "municipal" suggests, this court would be controlled by the city government of New York. The Washington, D.C. Municipal Court has the distinction of being a city court which is under federal jurisdiction because of the unique status of the District of Columbia.

2. **The correct answer is (D).** For the respective powers of the federal and state governments, look at Article One of the Constitution. Establishing post offices, issuing money, and conducting foreign relations are federal powers. Establishing schools is a state power. Federal and state governments share the power to establish banks, tax and borrow, establish courts, protect public health, and promote agriculture and industry.

3. **The correct answer is (D).** The Magna Carta, often described as one of the key documents in the evolution of democracy, was written in the thirteenth century and came before the Petition of Right in England. The Declaration of Independence obviously came before the Bill of Rights.

4. **The correct answer is (A).** The Fourteenth Amendment was of extreme importance to the development of civil liberties in the U.S. because it gave the federal government power over states. Thus, the phase "No State shall make or enforce..." should be recognizable to an AP Government student as belonging to the Fourteenth Amendment.

5. **The correct answer is (C).** The passage refers to slavery, and specifically to slaves who were moved from state to state. A significant point to take note of is that this language explicitly provides for slavery, in spite of the ideals stated in the Preamble to the Constitution which would seem to make slavery anathema.

6. **The correct answer is (C).** Double jeopardy is covered in the Fifth Amendment: "No person shall...be subject for the same offense to be twice put in jeopardy of life or limb."

7. **The correct answer is (B).** Joint committees are permanent committees that manage activities which concern both the House and Senate. Examples are the Joint Library Committee, the Joint Printing Committee, and Joint Economic Committee.

8. **The correct answer is (E).** PACs, which have increased in power and influence over the last two decades, raise the financial stakes of the election process by buying expensive television, radio, or newspaper ads for candidates they support (although they are limited by law in the amount of money they can contribute to any individual candidate's campaign).

9. **The correct answer is (E).** During the Reagan administration, both the majority leader of the Senate and the vice president were Republicans.

10. **The correct answer is (A).** The actual subject matter of *Marbury v. Madison*—last-minute appointments by a lame-duck president and a procedural error—were not important. Chief Justice Marshall established himself as a brilliant justice and increased the power of the Supreme Court by making itself the final arbiter in judging constitutionality. It also showed that federal employees could be held accountable in court and that statutes contrary to the Constitution were not valid.

11. **The correct answer is (B).** The Pendleton Act was written partly because of President Garfield's assassination, which was perpetrated by a disgruntled office seeker who did not get a civil service appointment. It was also written to eliminate the corruption which had arisen in previous administrations.

12. **The correct answer is (C).** The two key ways in which the Federal Reserve Board can influence the economy are through changing interest rates and manipulating the money supply. Although choice (B) might be conceivable in theory, it has never been a standard way of influencing the economy.

13. **The correct answer is (A).** Literacy requirements were deemed unconstitutional when it was discovered that such requirements were often used in the South as a way of discouraging minority voting.

14. **The correct answer is (A).** The Smith Act forbade actions or words that promoted the violent overthrow of the government. Since labor unions had traditionally contained communist and socialist elements, this made them suspect. One related controversy was whether or not union members should be required to take an oath that they would not abet or incite the violent overthrow of the government.

15. **The correct answer is (E).** As demonstrated by the phenomenon of "Reagan Democrats" and supporters for third-party candidates like Anderson and Perot, party loyalty is much weaker now than it was 50 years ago. This is not surprising since, in terms of benefits, parties currently provide much less for their members than they did years ago, when they would even provide aid for the needy.

16. **The correct answer is (D).** Charts and statistics can be deceptive. Notice on this chart that when added across, the percentages add up to 100 percent, but not when added down. The chart does not indicate an equal number of people in each of the four groups; it only tells you what the income breakdown is in each group. In other words, the Independents could number a total of 100 people and the Democrats could be numbered in the millions.

17. **The correct answer is (C).** Although choice (C) could very well be a correct hypothesis, it is not evinced by the hypothetical situation presented in this question.

18. **The correct answer is (C).** Even though in modern history the Democratic party has been a favorite of poor and minority groups, the Republican party was started as an antislavery party.

19. **The correct answer is (E).** Since many African American grandparents were slaves and obviously could not vote, a "grandfather clause" excluded African Americans from voting. The reason choice (A) is wrong is that previous to the "grandfather clauses," even white voters who were illiterate could vote.

20. **The correct answer is (B).** This excerpt from *Gitlow v. New York* had major significance because it expanded the power of the Fourteenth Amendment to cover states (and state subdivisions like cities), placing the interpretation of the First Amendment in the hands of the national government.

21. **The correct answer is (B).** A person convicted in a municipal court could have recourse by appealing to a federal court and be comforted to know that the federal court would have the final say on the issue.

22. **The correct answer is (E).** The Rules Committee clears major legislation, deciding when each piece goes to the House floor. The members of the committee are nominated by the Speaker of the House.

23. **The correct answer is (E).** Beginning with Jefferson refusing to spend $50,000 on gunboats, impoundment—the refusal to spend funds that Congress has appropriated—has been a way for the president to get around the fact that he holds no veto over congressional spending.

24. **The correct answer is (D).** To meet obvious national security needs, the president has been given sweeping powers over the military to be used in an emergency. Still, it is Congress that must formally declare war. The Executive Office pushed its power to use the military without a formal declaration of war by Congress to its limits during the conflict in Vietnam. The War Powers Resolution resulted from concerns that arose during the Vietnam War.

25. **The correct answer is (C).** The elitist theory professes that a small group of influential, wealthy people hold the significant power in Washington.

26. **The correct answer is (B).** Reagan in Grenada and Bush in the Persian Gulf seem to suggest that short, successful wars can raise a president's approval rating in the short run, especially if U.S. casualties are low. Longer conflicts with more casualties, like the Vietnam War, can often have the opposite effect.

27. **The correct answer is (A).** As questions of technology and the management of the budget become more complex, expertise in the executive branch becomes more important.

28. **The correct answer is (B).** The federal Department of Education does not have nearly as much authority as states when it comes to education. The Department of Education's

main avenue of influence is through the financial aid they provide to schools and the stipulations, such as student attendance, which they attach to the aid.

29. **The correct answer is (B).** The trend in lobbying has been to hire ex-government officials. These Washington insiders often have powerful connections, which is one key to effective lobbying, especially for clients like defense contractors who cannot boast of significant grass-roots support for political campaigns.

30. **The correct answer is (A).** The electoral college technically puts the final decision of who is elected president not in the hands of the people, but in the hands of a small group of specially selected representatives.

31. **The correct answer is (E).** Recent campaigns have shown that well-crafted commercials about a candidate and, sometimes more importantly, negative commercials about a political opponent are crucial to winning an election. Beyond this, a media consultant can also coach the candidate on how to look and act for any event which might have media coverage.

32. **The correct answer is (C).** Although it is not unusual for the executive branch to lobby for and against or to introduce legislation, it would not usually be involved in committee activities concerning a bill under consideration.

33. **The correct answer is (B).** Judicial restraint is applied by Supreme Court justices who feel that the judicial branch should not be so powerful and that the other branches of government, by virtue of the fact that they are elected and are therefore responsible to the people, should not be challenged too often by the Supreme Court.

34. **The correct answer is (D).** Treasury notes such as the one pictured for this question are a kind of security that the federal government issues to finance its deficits. When someone invests in such a note, he or she is loaning money to the government in exchange for interest payments. Similar securities are U.S. treasury bonds and treasury bills.

35. **The correct answer is (E).** The Fifteenth Amendment outlawed denying the right to vote because of "race, color, or previous condition of servitude." The Nineteenth Amendment gave women the right to vote. The Twenty-sixth Amendment gave 18-year-olds the right to vote. The Twentieth Amendment concerned the presidential term of office.

36. **The correct answer is (A).** Executive agreements do not require Senate ratification, but for all intents and purposes have the same effect as a treaty. The Congress has not approved of executive agreements, especially secret ones. The Case Act of 1972 placed restrictions on some agreements.

37. **The correct answer is (C).** Historically, businesses and manufacturers have opposed stringent environmental regulations on the grounds that they are expensive and make U.S. business less competitive in the international market.

38. **The correct answer is (C).** Threatening to veto or actually using the veto is a president's major formal influence over the legislative process. The Congress can override a veto, but it is usually not easy to garner enough votes for an override.

39. **The correct answer is (C).** When interpreting a political cartoon, always pay close attention to the written words. This is because a cartoonist will try to say as much as he/she can without using words. Therefore, whatever is written is usually essential. In this particular cartoon, the corpulence and unflattering aspects of the politician's representation strongly indicate a sarcastic interpretation of the label, "The 'Brains.'" Obviously, a person who has a money bag in place of a head can see and think of nothing but money.

40. **The correct answer is (E).** The Office of Technological Assessment was created in 1972 to confront the technical issues of energy and the environment.

41. **The correct answer is (C).** The Gulf of Tonkin Resolution stated "The United States is, therefore, prepared, as the president determines, to take all necessary steps, including the use of armed forces to assist any member or protocol state of the Southeast Asia Collective Defense Treaty requesting assistance in defense of its freedom." The clause "as the president determines" plainly gave President Johnson great power to deploy troops as he

saw fit without having to further worry about his congressional approval.

42. **The correct answer is (A)**. The New Deal programs that FDR used to help pull the U.S. out of the Great Depression created an unprecedented amount of government involvement in welfare, economy, health care, etc., which was never significantly reduced afterwards.

43. **The correct answer is (C)**. Spending excessive amounts of money on a candidate by a lobbyist would be considered unethical.

44. **The correct answer is (C)**. This quote is from *Bolling v. Sharpe*, which was considered at the same time *as Brown v. Board of Education of Topeka* and therefore shares the same precedent-changing view that separation of the races is inherently unequal.

45. **The correct answer is (D)**. Although this decision refuses to define liberty, it does relate the question of liberty to school segregation.

46. **The correct answer is (D)**. Since the one criticism of the Articles of Confederation was that the country as a whole was too weak and divided, the argument of a strong central government with the power to tax so that it could support a strong army was one that was used by Federalists as a reason to ratify the Constitution.

47. **The correct answer is (E)**. Even in the Articles of Confederation, which did not provide much power for the national government, the problems that could arise from states carrying on their own foreign policies were recognizes.

48. **The correct answer is (A)**. The Defense Department, with nearly one million employees, accounts for one-third of the total number of civilian employees working for the national government (not counting the 2.2 million military personnel).

49. **The correct answer is (D)**. Being a powerful member of the Appropriations Committee allows an individual the somewhat unsavory but politically helpful position of making sure that government projects spend a goodly sum in his/her home district. Although joint committees have members from both branches of Congress, none are as powerful as the big four: Appropriations, Armed Services, Finance, and Foreign Relations.

50. **The correct answer is (B)**. Relatively speaking, members of independent regulatory agencies are free from political fluctuations and survive changes in elected politicians. Cabinet appointees, for example, tend to change with each new administration. Senate and House staff members may or may not stay a long time depending on the political success of the congressperson for whom they work.

51. **The correct answer is (B)**. Industry deregulation and other policies of the Reagan era were generally designed to undo what the Republicans viewed as the evil of Democratic "tax and spend" liberalism.

52. **The correct answer is (E)**. Members of Congress now spend more than twice as much time serving the public than they did in the nineteenth century. It was considered a part-time job up until the early twentieth century, with the Congress meeting for less than six months out of the year.

53. **The correct answer is (D)**. The Court strongly influenced the economy most recently when it declared void parts of the Gramm-Rudman law, and as choice (D) states, after the Civil War, hearing cases that related to congressional and state laws regulating prices, wages, hours, working conditions, etc. Some examples of these cases were *Lochner v. New York*, where the Court struck down a law to set a maximum number of working hours, and *Muller v. Oregon*, where a statute setting the maximum number of working hours was upheld.

54. **The correct answer is (C)**. Most likely due to the prolonged recession (the economy can always be pointed to as a crucial factor for the incumbent president's popularity), foreign affairs took a back burner to domestic problems through most of the 1992 election campaign. Polls revealed that voters were more concerned with domestic issues when choosing a candidate.

55. **The correct answer is (D)**. There is no evidence or historical example suggesting that racial composition has made for more or less influence in a group. The great equalizer of current politics is that each person's

vote, regardless of race, is equally valued by public servants.

56. **The correct answer is (A).** The Kentucky and Virginia Resolutions, dated 1798, came after the framing of the Constitution and attacked a strong central government. The views expressed in these resolutions, written by Jefferson and Madison, were not the view that prevailed in the actual Constitution.

57. **The correct answer is (B).** Comparable worth advocates point to statistical evidence that women get paid less than men for jobs that are comparable in terms of demands and skill level, and that the government should regulate to correct this unfair practice. Arguments against comparable worth point out that trying to undo this wrong would be expensive and involve the government in private business to an undesirable degree.

58. **The correct answer is (C).** HUD has neither the will nor the finances to handle all local cases themselves. Since most states and municipalities have statutes that provide as much protection as the federal statutes, the first option is to let local authorities handle the case.

59. **The correct answer is (D).** The Simpson-Mazzoli Immigration Act allowed illegal aliens who had been in the United States for more than five years to apply for legal status. The majority of the immigrants who were affected were minorities, with Hispanics comprising the largest group.

60. **The correct answer is (E).** Named after a Massachusetts governor named Elbridge Gerry and the salamander, gerrymandering is the unethical practice of intentionally drawing district lines to enhance or diminish the reelection possibilities of a candidate or party.

PRACTICE TEST 2

Answer Sheet

1. Ⓐ Ⓑ Ⓒ Ⓓ Ⓔ	13. Ⓐ Ⓑ Ⓒ Ⓓ Ⓔ	25. Ⓐ Ⓑ Ⓒ Ⓓ Ⓔ	37. Ⓐ Ⓑ Ⓒ Ⓓ Ⓔ	49. Ⓐ Ⓑ Ⓒ Ⓓ Ⓔ
2. Ⓐ Ⓑ Ⓒ Ⓓ Ⓔ	14. Ⓐ Ⓑ Ⓒ Ⓓ Ⓔ	26. Ⓐ Ⓑ Ⓒ Ⓓ Ⓔ	38. Ⓐ Ⓑ Ⓒ Ⓓ Ⓔ	50. Ⓐ Ⓑ Ⓒ Ⓓ Ⓔ
3. Ⓐ Ⓑ Ⓒ Ⓓ Ⓔ	15. Ⓐ Ⓑ Ⓒ Ⓓ Ⓔ	27. Ⓐ Ⓑ Ⓒ Ⓓ Ⓔ	39. Ⓐ Ⓑ Ⓒ Ⓓ Ⓔ	51. Ⓐ Ⓑ Ⓒ Ⓓ Ⓔ
4. Ⓐ Ⓑ Ⓒ Ⓓ Ⓔ	16. Ⓐ Ⓑ Ⓒ Ⓓ Ⓔ	28. Ⓐ Ⓑ Ⓒ Ⓓ Ⓔ	40. Ⓐ Ⓑ Ⓒ Ⓓ Ⓔ	52. Ⓐ Ⓑ Ⓒ Ⓓ Ⓔ
5. Ⓐ Ⓑ Ⓒ Ⓓ Ⓔ	17. Ⓐ Ⓑ Ⓒ Ⓓ Ⓔ	29. Ⓐ Ⓑ Ⓒ Ⓓ Ⓔ	41. Ⓐ Ⓑ Ⓒ Ⓓ Ⓔ	53. Ⓐ Ⓑ Ⓒ Ⓓ Ⓔ
6. Ⓐ Ⓑ Ⓒ Ⓓ Ⓔ	18. Ⓐ Ⓑ Ⓒ Ⓓ Ⓔ	30. Ⓐ Ⓑ Ⓒ Ⓓ Ⓔ	42. Ⓐ Ⓑ Ⓒ Ⓓ Ⓔ	54. Ⓐ Ⓑ Ⓒ Ⓓ Ⓔ
7. Ⓐ Ⓑ Ⓒ Ⓓ Ⓔ	19. Ⓐ Ⓑ Ⓒ Ⓓ Ⓔ	31. Ⓐ Ⓑ Ⓒ Ⓓ Ⓔ	43. Ⓐ Ⓑ Ⓒ Ⓓ Ⓔ	55. Ⓐ Ⓑ Ⓒ Ⓓ Ⓔ
8. Ⓐ Ⓑ Ⓒ Ⓓ Ⓔ	20. Ⓐ Ⓑ Ⓒ Ⓓ Ⓔ	32. Ⓐ Ⓑ Ⓒ Ⓓ Ⓔ	44. Ⓐ Ⓑ Ⓒ Ⓓ Ⓔ	56. Ⓐ Ⓑ Ⓒ Ⓓ Ⓔ
9. Ⓐ Ⓑ Ⓒ Ⓓ Ⓔ	21. Ⓐ Ⓑ Ⓒ Ⓓ Ⓔ	33. Ⓐ Ⓑ Ⓒ Ⓓ Ⓔ	45. Ⓐ Ⓑ Ⓒ Ⓓ Ⓔ	57. Ⓐ Ⓑ Ⓒ Ⓓ Ⓔ
10. Ⓐ Ⓑ Ⓒ Ⓓ Ⓔ	22. Ⓐ Ⓑ Ⓒ Ⓓ Ⓔ	34. Ⓐ Ⓑ Ⓒ Ⓓ Ⓔ	46. Ⓐ Ⓑ Ⓒ Ⓓ Ⓔ	58. Ⓐ Ⓑ Ⓒ Ⓓ Ⓔ
11. Ⓐ Ⓑ Ⓒ Ⓓ Ⓔ	23. Ⓐ Ⓑ Ⓒ Ⓓ Ⓔ	35. Ⓐ Ⓑ Ⓒ Ⓓ Ⓔ	47. Ⓐ Ⓑ Ⓒ Ⓓ Ⓔ	59. Ⓐ Ⓑ Ⓒ Ⓓ Ⓔ
12. Ⓐ Ⓑ Ⓒ Ⓓ Ⓔ	24. Ⓐ Ⓑ Ⓒ Ⓓ Ⓔ	36. Ⓐ Ⓑ Ⓒ Ⓓ Ⓔ	48. Ⓐ Ⓑ Ⓒ Ⓓ Ⓔ	60. Ⓐ Ⓑ Ⓒ Ⓓ Ⓔ

GO ON TO THE NEXT PAGE

Practice Test 2

UNITED STATES GOVERNMENT AND POLITICS

Multiple Choice

Time—45 Minutes

60 Questions

Directions: *Each of the questions or incomplete statements below is followed by five possible answer choices. Select the one choice that best answers the question or completes the statement and fill in the corresponding oval on the answer sheet.*

1. The quotation that follows contains a point of view that was expressed at the Constitutional Convention. Read the quote and decide which of the ideas incorporated into the Constitution most closely expresses the same viewpoint.

   "...The people are turbulent and changing: they seldom judge or determine right. Give therefore to the [upper] class a permanent share in the government. They will check the unsteadiness of the [lower], and as they cannot receive any advantage by a change, they will ever maintain good government..."

   (A) the First Amendment
   (B) the electoral college
   (C) judicial review
   (D) the elastic clause
   (E) the bicameral system with a Senate

2. Which of the following would be the most effective technique for the federal government to control inflation?
   (A) reducing federal interest rates
   (B) increasing income taxes for the middle class
   (C) increasing income taxes for the wealthy
   (D) lowering Social Security benefits
   (E) repealing luxury surtaxes

3. The most important factor influencing foreign policy decisions is
   (A) friendships among leaders of nations
   (B) imperialist inclinations
   (C) public reaction
   (D) racial composition of the foreign country
   (E) national self-interest

4. The double jeopardy clause of the federal Constitution protects the civil liberties of an individual by
   (A) requiring that at least two witnesses defend the accused in a juried trial
   (B) prohibiting family members of a convicted criminal from being punished for his or her crime
   (C) making it illegal for a person to be arrested without first being read his or her rights
   (D) preventing an acquitted defendant from being tried twice for the same criminal charge
   (E) giving a criminal defendant the right not to testify against himself or herself

5. Which of the following actions taken by President Abraham Lincoln during his tenure as president was based on a presidential power explicitly laid out in the Constitution?
   (A) consult with the Rules Committee of Congress frequently
   (B) issue the Emancipation Proclamation
   (C) remove General McClellan as commander of the Army of the Potomac
   (D) formulate the "10 percent" plan of Reconstruction
   (E) visit various states in the Union

6. Which of the following was an important reason for dissatisfaction with the Articles of Confederation among the merchant class?
   (A) Congress had unlimited power to tax.
   (B) The president's power to make treaties could not be checked by the other branches of government.

GO ON TO THE NEXT PAGE

(C) Business was hampered by state regulation of commerce.
(D) Congress was not allowed to set up a national monetary system.
(E) Federal taxes were extremely high.

7. The key element of the Great Compromise that made the Constitution acceptable to opposing interests in the United States was
(A) a federal judicial system with a Supreme Court
(B) a Bill of Rights
(C) a bicameral system of government where the House of Representatives members are selected by population size and the Senate members provide equal representation for each state
(D) the eventual prohibition of slavery would take place 20 years after the signing of the Constitution
(E) state legislators would always have the power to veto unpopular federal legislation

8. An example of the concurrent powers of states and the national government is the right to
(A) levy taxes
(B) declare war
(C) suspend the writ of habeas corpus
(D) coin money
(E) control interstate commerce

9. The procedures involved in amending the Constitution
(A) have played a significant but relatively limited role in adapting the Constitution to changing conditions
(B) are so difficult that they have been of little importance
(C) are so easy that they have been used too often
(D) have been used only to protect the civil rights of the people
(E) have been changed and adjusted to adapt to an evolving government

10. The elastic clause contained in Article One, Section 8, clause 18 of the Constitution gives the Congress power to
(A) do anything necessary to benefit the general welfare
(B) carry out expressed powers specifically granted by the Constitution
(C) approve treaties with foreign nations
(D) act as a check on the power of the other two branches of government
(E) raise and lower taxes as the economy and the expenses incurred by the national government necessitate

11. Investigative committees most often serve the purpose of
(A) supplying the basis for legislation
(B) gathering evidence concerning the violation of laws
(C) trying to reach compromises to settle conflicts between the Senate and the House
(D) creating media attention for important legislative issues
(E) looking into improprieties in the executive and judicial branches of government

12. Which of the following checks on the president's powers is "unwritten" rather than specifically stated by the Constitution?
(A) Congress's right to override a veto if they have a two-thirds majority of votes
(B) Senate's approval of appointments
(C) Senate's right to approve treaties
(D) senatorial courtesy
(E) Congress's "power of the purse"

13. In a hypothetical election with three major candidates, what would happen if the electoral vote distribution was as follows:
Candidate A: 255
Candidate B: 174
Candidate C: 109
(A) candidate A would win the election and become the next president
(B) the House of Representatives would choose between the three candidates
(C) the House of Representatives would choose between candidates A and B
(D) candidates A and B would participate in a run-off election
(E) candidate A would become president and candidate B would become vice president

14. The Supreme Court would be given original jurisdiction in which of the following cases?
    (A) A citizen files a suit against local authorities saying that his or her civil rights have been violated.
    (B) A citizen is charged with violating federal income tax codes.
    (C) Several men have been accused of robbing a local bank.
    (D) Some youngsters are accused of vandalizing a national park.
    (E) New Jersey files a suit against New York State involving navigation rights on the Hudson River.

15. Five weeks after a couple is married in one state they become residents of a different state. Which of the following statements about the legality of their marital status is true?
    (A) The marriage certificate has to be reissued in the new state, but the new state is not allowed to charge the newly married couple for the service.
    (B) The marriage certificate is not valid in any other state.
    (C) Marriage, like divorce, is recognized in some states but not in others.
    (D) The full faith and credit clause in Article Four, Section 1 of the Constitution requires that the new state in which they become residents honor their marriage.
    (E) Article Four, Section 2 of the Constitution guarantees that the new state to which the recently married couple moved will recognize the marriage as legal.

16. All of the following Bill of Rights Amendments, Supreme Court Cases and descriptions are grouped accurately EXCEPT
    (A) First Amendment, freedom of speech, *Gitlow v. New York*
    (B) Fourth Amendment, exclusionary rule, *Mapp v. Ohio*
    (C) Fourth Amendment, protection from unreasonable searches and seizures, *Wolf v. Ohio*
    (D) Fifth Amendment, prohibition of double jeopardy, *Bakke v. University of California*
    (E) First Amendment, freedom of press, *Near v. Minnesota*

17. Based on the message being portrayed in the above political cartoon of Andrew Jackson, which of the following statements is most accurate?
    (A) President Jackson had total disregard for the Constitution.
    (B) President Jackson used his veto power as an important tool of his presidency.
    (C) President Jackson often dressed and acted more like a king than a president.
    (D) President Jackson walked all over the Constitution of the United States but supported the Internal Improvements Bank.
    (E) President Jackson was a champion of the common man.

18. All of the following convinced the framers of the Constitution to establish a Congress with two branches EXCEPT
    (A) A compromise between the Virginia and New Jersey Plans could be reached by creating a bicameral Congress.
    (B) A bicameral Congress would create an internal check on the power of the legislative branch.

GO ON TO THE NEXT PAGE

(C) The precedent of bicameralism was already set in the Articles of Confederation.
(D) Most Colonial Assemblies and the British Parliament were bicameral.
(E) Bicameralism was supported by the ideas of John Locke.

19. Which of the following components of the Constitution is supported by this excerpt from Madison's *Federalist No. 52*?

"As it is essential to liberty that the government in general should have a common interest with the people, so it is particularly essential that the [House of Representatives] should have an immediate dependence on, and an intimate sympathy with, the people. Frequent elections are unquestionably the only policy by which this dependence and sympathy can be effectively secured."

(A) Impeachment procedures can be put into motion by ordinary citizens.
(B) The First Amendment, which provides the people with a common interest.
(C) A bicameral system keeps the House of Representatives from becoming too strong.
(D) A system of two-year elections for members of the House of Representatives.
(E) A greater amount of power for representatives than for senators.

20. All of the following reasons help explain why such a high percentage of incumbents get reelected to Congress EXCEPT
(A) their campaigns receive a greater share of federal matching funds
(B) their staffs can help incumbents' constituents deal with the government
(C) they can win constituent support by providing pork-barrel projects for the district they represent
(D) free mailing and media opportunities provide greater name recognition for incumbents
(E) PACs are more likely to support incumbents

21. Which of the following is a feature of the ethics code written by the Senate and House of Representatives?
(A) Members of Congress can keep up to $4,000 earned for speeches and public appearances.
(B) Members of the Senate may keep up to 60 percent of their outside income.
(C) Members of Congress keep up to 50 percent of their yearly congressional salaries as honoraria.
(D) Every member of Congress has to file a financial disclosure statement annually.
(E) Members of neither house are allowed to buy any government issued tax-free bonds.

22. All of the following explain why the Speaker of the House is the most powerful legislator in Washington EXCEPT
(A) The Speaker refers bills to committees.
(B) The Speaker rules on questions of parliamentary procedure.
(C) The Speaker decides who will be recognized to speak on the House floor.
(D) The Speaker appoints members of select and conference committees.
(E) The Speaker selects chairpersons of standing committees.

23. Which of the following changes reduced the power of committee chairpersons in the 1970s?
(A) staff members are guaranteed seats on some committees
(B) no members of Congress can chair more than one committee
(C) committee chairpersons are elected by party majority rather than chosen solely on the basis of seniority
(D) all committee and subcommittee meetings must be open to the public unless, in an open-session meeting, it is decided to close the meeting
(E) all of the above

24. All the following statements about riders on amendments that have reached the Senate floor are true EXCEPT
(A) Riders are often attached to appropriations measures.

(B) A bill stalled in committee is sometimes called an amendment, so that it can get onto the Senate floor.

(C) The president and Congress might approve a rider that they are against because it is attached to a popular bill.

(D) The Supreme Court is often forced to step in and prevent the passage of such amendments because they are unconstitutional.

(E) Many riders are not related in subject to the amendment.

25. Which of the following is a power that Congress has over foreign policy?

(A) to fire and hire ambassadors

(B) to appoint the commander in chief of the armed forces

(C) to refuse to provide aid to a foreign country

(D) to arrest ambassadors from foreign countries

(E) to select the secretary of state

26. Which of the following powers belong to the vice president?

I. to succeed a president who dies, resigns, or is impeached

II. to help decide whether or not the president is disabled

III. to act as the president's chief representative in foreign countries

IV. to cast tie-breaking voters in the Senate

(A) I, II

(B) I, IV

(C) I, II, IV

(D) II, III, IV

(E) I, II, III, IV

Questions 27–28 refer to the following list:

vice president
Speaker of the House
president pro tempore of the Senate
secretary of state
secretary of the treasury
secretary of defense
attorney general
secretary of the interior
secretary of agriculture
secretary of commerce
secretary of labor
secretary of health and human services
secretary of housing and urban development
secretary of transportation
secretary of energy
secretary of education
secretary of veterans' affairs

27. What is this a list of?

(A) offices appointed by the president

(B) members of the cabinet

(C) the presidential line of succession

(D) the most powerful politicians in Washington

(E) jobs that have never been filled by women

28. The list can be most accurately described as

(A) in descending order, the most to the least powerful politicians in Washington

(B) containing members of a variety of political affiliations and background qualifications

(C) all members of the same party

(D) all occupying positions that are called for in the Constitution

(E) the least influential people in Washington

29. Which of the following are valid criticisms of presidential primaries?

I. The public and candidates get tired of the lengthening election campaigns.

II. Primaries make elections more expensive.

III. The best candidates seldom win in the primaries.

IV. Primaries do more to divide a party than unite it.

(A) I, II, III, IV

(B) I, II

(C) III, IV

(D) I, II, IV

(E) I, II, III

GO ON TO THE NEXT PAGE

30. Read the following quote from George Mason, a member of the Constitutional Convention, and decide which of the following features of the Constitution reflects the ideas expressed in the quote.

"It would be as unnatural to refer the choice of a proper character for chief magistrate to the people, as it would be to refer a trial of colors to a blind man. The extent of the Country renders it impossible that the people can have the requisite capacity to judge of the respective pretensions of the Candidates."

(A) electoral college
(B) the Senate with equal representation from each state
(C) a federal department of education
(D) presidential primaries
(E) government sponsored debates

31. Under which conditions may police legally invade the security of someone's private home?

(A) when an emergency develops that demands immediate attention, such a fire or an explosion
(B) if a criminal suspect who the police are pursuing enters the private home
(C) when they have a valid search warrant
(D) if the occupant of the home invites them in
(E) all of the conditions stated above

Questions 32–33 are based on the following hypothetical political speech:

"Our government in its present manifestation does not come close to meeting the needs of the proletariat. The basic structures of government which pit race against race, rich against poor, city folk against country folk are jaded, jaundiced, and a curse on one of the richest countries in the world. It is fine to criticize the government in halls such as this one or in living rooms or across dining room tables, but that in the end is a fruitless endeavor. It is for this reason I am pleading with you to, in the spirit of our forefathers who shed their blood to win this country's independence from a tyrant, take arms immediately. One less politician who is in bed with millionaire oppressors is one step closer to reaching our goal of government for the people and by the people."

32. What explains why the above speech given at a hypothetical political rally might be considered cause enough for arrest of the speaker?

(A) it is obscene
(B) it violates common standards of public morality
(C) it promotes a foreign system of government
(D) it presents a clear-and-present danger
(E) all the reasons stated above

33. Which of the following government actions is most closely related to the above speech?

(A) the Pendleton Act
(B) the Miranda decision
(C) the War Powers Act
(D) the Smith Act
(E) the Bakke decision

34. The political parties that could be considered the closest ancestors to the modern Republican party are the

(A) Progressive and State Rights parties
(B) Federalists and Whigs
(C) Democratic-Republicans and Federalists
(D) Antifederalists and the American Independent party
(E) none of these

35. All of the following have been true about third parties EXCEPT

(A) Their ideas have often been absorbed by the bigger parties.
(B) They often have a narrow set of issues which they rally around.
(C) They often get weaker as the actual election draws near.
(D) All the states have basically the same procedure for putting them on the ballot.
(E) The Republican party began as a small party catering mostly to sectional interests.

Presidential Approval Rating by Interest Group
Percentage out of 100% Up to 4% Sampling error on mounthly polls

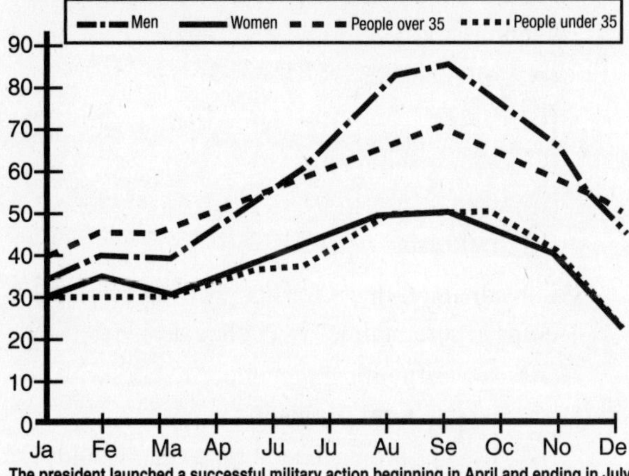

The president launched a successful military action beginning in April and ending in July

36. What statement is most valid based upon the information given in the above graph?
   (A) The military action improved the president's approval rating for each of the groups included.
   (B) A president tends to lose popularity the longer he is in office.
   (C) Members of the same interest group were unanimous in their views on a given issue.
   (D) Domestic issues were more likely to change people's opinions than foreign issues.
   (E) Women were more likely to side with younger voters than older ones.

37. Which of the following actions would most likely be supported by a politician who is considered to be a fiscal conservative?
   (A) a socialized system of health care modeled after Britain or Canada
   (B) less government environmental restrictions on businesses
   (C) a government jobs program that guarantees everyone an opportunity for employment
   (D) an increase in minimum wage
   (E) more government money spent on research and incentives for business

38. Which political label best describes the majority of U.S. voters?
   (A) moderate
   (B) liberal
   (C) conservative
   (D) reactionary
   (E) right wing

39. Which is the most likely reason why voters who consider themselves to be independent often register with a political party?
   (A) They could not otherwise vote in general elections.
   (B) Party primaries are an important part of the election process.
   (C) A voter has to vote in the primary in order to vote in the general election.
   (D) The Constitution forbids people to register as independents.
   (E) Peer pressure to join a political party has historically been extremely important.

40. What percentage of eligible voters usually vote in U.S. general elections?
   (A) 40 percent
   (B) 60 percent
   (C) 80 percent
   (D) 90 percent
   (E) 20 percent

41. Which of the following cross sections of people would produce the most accurate poll results?
   (A) a straw poll taken among people actively working on political campaigns for a variety of candidates
   (B) a random sampling of people in a mall
   (C) a cross sampling of people from a variety of geographical locations and a variety of income groups
   (D) a large sampling of people in the media
   (E) a cross sampling of people in three cities from three different geographical locations

42. Which of the following would most likely be decided upon using a referendum?
   (A) a bill appropriating money for interstate highway renovation
   (B) a president election where the victor won by only 50 electoral college votes
   (C) a bill about employee insurance requirements for business
   (D) a bond proposal to raise money for schools
   (E) a deadlocked Supreme Court nomination

GO ON TO THE NEXT PAGE

43. What is the most common criticism of federal aid to schools by educators?
    (A) it is usually not needed and creates useless paperwork
    (B) private schools get a disproportionate amount of the money
    (C) it forces schools to adopt the Judeo-Christian value system
    (D) the money often comes by sacrificing the military budget
    (E) the money often has strings attached, such as performance standards or school attendance

44. The correct path for a case in the federal courts would be
    (A) from a U.S. district court to a U.S. court of appeals to the U.S. Supreme Court
    (B) from a small claims court to a U.S. district court to a court of claims
    (C) form the U.S. Supreme Court to a state supreme court to a court of appeals
    (D) from a court of claims to a customs court to the Federal Circuit Court of Appeals
    (E) from the Court of Military Appeals to the U.S. Supreme Court to a U.S. court of appeals

45. One way that the Securities and Exchange Commission protects investors is
    (A) taking stock-trading privileges away from companies that might lose money
    (B) requiring companies that issue securities to disclose financial information
    (C) taking over the management and day-to-day operations of insolvent companies
    (D) buying and selling stock in order to stabilize the prices
    (E) making sure that neither itself nor any other government agency tries to influence the stock market

46. Which agency would hold hearings concerning the raising of phone rates?
    (A) Interstate Commerce Commission
    (B) Civil Aeronautics Board
    (C) Federal Communications Commission
    (D) Community Services Administration
    (E) Postal Rate Commission

47. Which method of interstate transport is not regulated by the Interstate Commerce Commission?
    (A) oil pipelines
    (B) trucks
    (C) canals and rivers
    (D) cars
    (E) railroads

48. Subsidizing farmers for not growing certain crops at certain times is a policy designed to
    (A) reward political supporters in states with a large farm population
    (B) use up surplus federal funds that would otherwise be lost
    (C) create a stockpile of surplus food staples that can be used in times of emergency
    (D) help foreign competitors
    (E) maintain farm prices at a profitable level by eliminating excessive surpluses

49. What is an effective way for the House of Representatives and the Senate to influence the direction of foreign policy that the president is following?
    (A) reject treaties signed by the president
    (B) file a court injunction
    (C) carry on separate negotiations with a foreign country
    (D) suspend or cut off monetary support
    (E) hold hearings to rally public support

50. Which best describes Congress's fiscal policy in the 1980s?
    (A) diminished pork-barrel politics
    (B) elimination of tax loopholes for the lower and upper classes
    (C) deficit spending
    (D) tax incentives to invest in foreign countries
    (E) fiscal restraint

GO ON TO THE NEXT PAGE

51. "Neither a state nor the federal government can set up a church. Neither can they pass laws which aid one religion, aid all religions, or prefer one religion over another. Neither can they force...a person to go to or to remain away from church against his will, or force him to profess a belief or disbelief in any religion."

The above decision by Justice Hugo Black from *Everson v. Board of Education* created which of the following precedents?

(A) "separate but equal"
(B) establishment clause
(C) free exercise clause
(D) religious freedom clause
(E) integration clause

52. What case established some limits on the First Amendment guarantee to worship freely?

(A) *Wisconsin v. Yoder*
(B) *Reynolds v. United States*
(C) *Sherbert v. Verner*
(D) *Engel v. Vitale*
(E) *Widmer v. Vincent*

53. Keeping legal precedents in mind, which of the following cases would most likely be successful?

(A) a politician suing a newspaper for printing unsubstantiated rumors that he is a spy for a foreign country
(B) a newspaper being sued for running an advertisement criticizing a police chief for terrifying minority groups
(C) a TV news anchorperson being sued for reporting unsubstantiated rumors that a politician had an affair
(D) a magazine editor being sued for publishing personal attacks by one candidate for office against another
(E) a reporter being sued by a military general for reporting that the general misrepresented the facts of a battle to the president

54. The term "prior restraint" would most likely be used in which of the following actions?

(A) arrest
(B) amnesty
(C) censorship
(D) sentencing for a crime
(E) a court appeal

55. All of the following amendments protect the right of due process EXCEPT

(A) Fourth Amendment
(B) Fifth Amendment
(C) Sixth Amendment
(D) Eighth Amendment
(E) Tenth Amendment

56. Which of the following could be considered a zone of privacy off-limits to government interference.

(A) thoughts and beliefs
(B) personal information
(C) family and personal relationships
(D) choices A, B, and C
(E) none of the choices given

57. Which of the following civil rights landmarks does not fit with the other four?

(A) *Dred Scott v. Sandford*
(B) Fourteenth Amendment
(C) Fifteenth Amendment
(D) Civil Rights Act of 1866
(E) Civil Rights Act of 1975

58. The institution of slavery and the dearth of civil rights for blacks and women in early U.S. history could be best described as resulting from

(A) basic flaws in the ideas behind the Constitution
(B) discriminatory tendencies by the people who acted on and interpreted the Constitution
(C) the desire by the majority of the country to unify the country at all costs
(D) unreasonable demands by African-Americans
(E) the difficulty involved in amending the Constitution

59. All of the following are provisions in the Civil Rights Act of 1964 EXCEPT

(A) bars arbitrary discrimination in voter registration
(B) outlaws discrimination in public accommodations
(C) explicitly outlaws reverse discrimination
(D) prohibits job discrimination
(E) expands the power of the Civil Rights Commission

GO ON TO THE NEXT PAGE

60. The statement "You do not take a person who for years has been hobbled by chains and liberate him, bring him up to the starting line of the race, and then say, 'you are free to compete with all the others,' and still justly believe that you have been completely fair. Thus it is not enough to open the gates of opportunity. All of our citizens must walk through those gates" can most reasonably be linked to
   (A) *Korematsu v. U.S.*
   (B) *Brown v. Board of Education of Topeka*
   (C) reverse discrimination
   (D) affirmative action
   (E) "separate but equal"

STOP

THIS IS THE END OF THIS SECTION. YOU MAY CHECK YOUR ANSWERS IN THIS SECTION IF THERE IS EXTRA TIME REMAINING.

PRACTICE TEST 2

Quick-Score Answer Key

1.	B	21.	D	41.	C
2.	A	22.	E	42.	D
3.	E	23.	E	43.	E
4.	D	24.	D	44.	A
5.	C	25.	C	45.	B
6.	C	26.	C	46.	C
7.	C	27.	C	47.	D
8.	A	28.	B	48.	E
9.	A	29.	B	49.	D
10.	B	30.	A	50.	C
11.	A	31.	E	51.	B
12.	D	32.	D	52.	B
13.	B	33.	D	53.	A
14.	E	34.	B	54.	C
15.	E	35.	D	55.	E
16.	D	36.	E	56.	D
17.	B	37.	B	57.	A
18.	C	38.	A	58.	B
19.	D	39.	B	59.	C
20.	A	40.	B	60.	D

PRACTICE TEST 2—EXPLANATORY ANSWERS

1. **The correct answer is (B).** The electoral college system is a system where electors previously named by political parties make the final selection for president. A certain number is assigned to each state. The only explanation for the electoral college, since it is a system which is more cumbersome and less democratic than a direct vote, is that the framers of the Constitution did not trust the common man to be able to make the proper decision at all times.

2. **The correct answer is (A).** Reducing federal interest rates causes private banks to do the same. This is one of the most effective and speediest ways that the federal government has to influence the economy. Although the results of lowering or raising interest rates are not 100 percent predictable, it has generally proven to be a useful technique.

3. **The correct answer is (E).** Whether or not politicians explicitly say so, national self-interest is the overriding consideration in conducting foreign affairs. History shows that the U.S. is most likely to take military action against a foreign country if what it does directly affects the economy or other interests of the U.S. A problem arises when politicians and/or citizens disagree about what our national self-interest is. For example, a pacifist might argue that in the long run, war is never in our self-interest, while many others would say that practically speaking, war is sometimes necessary.

4. **The correct answer is (D).** The Fifth Amendment to the Constitution states, "nor shall any person be subject for the same offense to be twice put in jeopardy of life or limb."

5. **The correct answer is(C).** Article Two, Section 2 of the Constitution states, "The President shall be Commander in Chief of the Army and Navy of the United States, and of the militia of the several States, when called into the actual service of the United States...." The role of commander in chief provides the president with sweeping power to coordinate the military, and that includes dismissing the military when necessary. Compare this to the president's relative lack of authority when it comes to disciplining other members of government.

6. **The correct answer is (C).** One of the numerous problems with the Articles of Confederation was the lack of centralized control over interstate commerce. Each state acted like a foreign country in terms of tariffs and duties levied on products passing between states.

7. **The correct answer is (C).** The Great Compromise, sometimes called the Connecticut Compromise, combined the Virginia Plan of representation by population in the House of Representatives and the New Jersey Plan of equal representation in the Senate.

8. **The correct answer is (A).** Concurrent powers, as opposed to denied or reserved powers, are powers that states and the federal government share. As all taxpayers are aware, the federal, state, and even municipal governments can levy taxes.

9. **The correct answer is (A).** One only has to look at the fact that there have been less than 30 amendments over the history of the United States to conclude that the passing of amendments has been limited. On the other hand, if one looks at the changes brought on by amendments, their importance cannot be denied.

10. **The correct answer is (B).** The elastic clause does not create new power. As its name suggests, it allows Congress to expand its power when necessary, but only to control areas explicitly set out in the Constitution. The clause reads, "To make all laws which shall be necessary and proper for carrying into execution the foregoing powers, and all other powers vested by this Constitution in the Government of the United States, or in any department or officer thereof." In general, judicial decisions have buffeted Congress's expansion under the elastic clause.

11. **The correct answer is (A).** Investigative committees gather information, as well as research the need, feasibility, and public opinion concerning proposed legislation.

12. **The correct answer is (D).** Senatorial courtesy is a custom, not a written component of the Constitution, which allows a senator from the same party as the president to block an appointment from his or her own state.

13. **The correct answer is (B).** The number of electors is the number of representatives and senators, plus three for the District of Columbia (see the Twenty-third Amendment). To become president, the candidate must receive a majority of electoral votes. If this does not happen, then the House of Representatives chooses from among the top three finishers. Each state would have one vote.

14. **The correct answer is (E).** Original jurisdiction is spelled out in Article Three of the Constitution and includes four kinds of disputes: cases between one of the states and the United States government; cases between two or more states; cases involving foreign ambassadors, ministers, or consuls; and cases begun by a state against a citizen of another state or against another country.

15. **The correct answer is (E).** Article Four, Section 2 of the Constitution states, "The citizens of each State shall be entitled to all privileges and immunities of citizens in the several States." This includes marriage.

16. **The correct answer is (D).** The Bakke case involved a white student who sued a university claiming reverse discrimination. He won the case in 1978. This decision was a blow against quotas as a method of fostering racial equality.

17. **The correct answer is (B).** The veto in his hand and the "of veto memory" written on the side informs you that Jackson's use of veto is central to this cartoon. The writing, "born to command," "had I been consulted," and "King Andrew the First," creates the idea that Andrew Jackson wielded "imperial" power when it came to using vetoes. Choice (E), although historically valid, is not supported by this cartoon.

18. **The correct answer is (C).** The Articles of Confederation created a one-house legislature with delegations ranging from two to seven members.

19. **The correct answer is (D).** "Frequent elections" from the excerpt of Madison's essay supports two-year elections.

20. **The correct answer is (A).** Legally speaking, matching funds are as readily attainable by outsiders as incumbents. However, the other factors mentioned, which are in favor of incumbents, occasionally prevent challengers from getting as far in their campaigns.

21. **The correct answer is (D).** Congress is exempt from many laws from which common citizens are not exempt. Both houses of Congress have drawn up their own code of ethics, including financial disclosures, which average citizens would consider an affront to their civil liberties.

22. **The correct answer is (E).** Chairpersons of standing committees are selected according to party and seniority.

23. **The correct answer is (E).** This question should serve as a reminder that before you jump to an answer, you should consider each choice. In fact, the process of elimination is the best way to go about a multiple-choice test. In this case, if you knew that at least two of the choices were correct, then you could confidently answer choice (E).

24. **The correct answer is (D).** Although riders are often distasteful and suggest "back room" dealing, the Supreme Court has never taken such an active role in the legislative process.

25. **The correct answer is (C).** Article One, Section 8 of the Constitution says, "Congress shall have power to lay and collect taxes, duties, imposts, and excises, to pay the debts and provide for the common defense and general welfare of the United States," as well as, "To regulate commerce with foreign nations, and among the several States, and with the Indian tribes." For example, the Iran-Contra affair came when the executive branch disobeyed Congress's decision to stop aiding the Contras in their fight against the government of Nicaragua.

26. **The correct answer is (C).** The secretary of state acts as the president's chief foreign emissary. Many have criticized the position of vice president as not being useful.

27. **The correct answer is (C).** Most students are familiar with the first four names in the presidential line of succession, but not the names on the bottom of the list. The line of succession was created by the Succession Act of 1947.

28. **The correct answer is (B).** Whereas the vice president, Speaker of the House, and president pro tempore of the Senate are elected officials, the cabinet heads are often appointed for their expertise in a certain area.

29. **The correct answer is (B).** Statement III is an opinion that one might hear expressed, but it is too conjectural to makc a strong argument for it. Statement IV would also be difficult to support with a logical argument, since a historical view of primaries shows that even the ones most strongly contested do not necessarily weaken the party.

30. **The correct answer is (A).** This quote from George Mason reflects what some might now call an elitist attitude, which rejected direct democracy for fear that the common people would not be able to make informed selections. This was the main reason for the electoral college.

31. **The correct answer is (E).** Choices (A) through (D) are all exceptions to the common liberty protections against unlawful search and seizure.

32. **The correct answer is (D).** The formula of clear-and-present danger was written by Justice Oliver Wendell Holmes. The gist of it is that there must be a clear-and-present danger to public safety or national security before the government can move to restrict any freedoms guaranteed by the Constitution. The last three lines of this hypothetical political speech suggest that people should use violence to eliminate politicians. The danger that could arise if the audience listening to the speech were to act upon it supersedes the rights of free speech normally enjoyed by U.S. citizens.

33. **The correct answer is (D).** The Smith Act of 1940, written at a time when the "Red Scare" was prevalent, made it illegal for any person to teach or advocate the violent overthrow of the government.

34. **The correct answer is (B).** The Republican party can be traced all the way back to the Federalists. It later broke up and was replaced by the National Republican party in the early 1800s. This party did not last long—it was absorbed by the Whig party in the1830s.

35. **The correct answer is (D).** States vary in their procedures for putting candidates on the ballot. Differences in the number of signatures on a petition, the deadlines for filling, and the steps needed to maintain a candidate's eligibility for remaining on the ballot cause some states to have more third-party candidates than others in a typical election.

36. **The correct answer is (E).** The fact that the shift in the opinion ratings for these two groups went up and down at the same time supports choice (E). When answering this kind of graph question, be sure to read the label on the map and the parameters carefully.

37. **The correct answer is (B).** A fiscal conservative—someone who follows conservative policies when it comes to the economy—generally wants less government interference, and the record shows that this includes fewer government environmental restrictions.

38. **The correct answer is (A).** Recent surveys have shown that the majority of U.S. voters in recent elections describe themselves as moderate.

39. **The correct answer is (B).** Political primaries offer a larger number of candidates with more varied ideas than does the general election, which usually offers only two viable candidates.

40. **The correct answer is (B).** The actual figure has been closer to 55 percent. This figure is much lower than that of other democracies. A difficult registration procedure, voter alienation, one-party domination, and complex election issues are some reasons given for this low turnout.

41. **The correct answer is (C).** In general, pollsters try to poll a broad spectrum of people with a broad variety of ethnic, geographical, and financial backgrounds.

42. **The correct answer is (D).** Bond elections, like amendments to state constitutions in all states except Delaware, require mandatory referendums by law.

43. **The correct answer is (E).** Many educators feel that the requirements often tied to the receiving of aid take away from local autonomy, and often amount to unnecessary bureaucracy and federal interference.

44. **The correct answer is (A).** The hierarchy of federal court jurisdiction starts in small local courts, progresses through the appeals process, and finally stops at the U.S. Supreme Court. The basic logic behind the system is to save the U.S. Supreme Court for important decisions. Two basic routes to the U.S. Supreme Court are through municipal courts and then to the state supreme court, or through U.S. district courts, courts of claims, customs court, and then to the U.S. court of appeals.

45. **The correct answer is (B).** The Securities and Exchange Commission was conceived as a consumer protection agency to help keep investors safe from unscrupulous companies. Besides demanding financial disclosures, the SEC sets controls on margin buying, the futures market, holding companies, mutual funds, and the stock market.

46. **The correct answer is (C).** The FCC licenses the use of public airwaves, sets standards for broadcasting, and also holds hearings on telephone rates.

47. **The correct answer is (D).** The ICC regulates transport in order to make sure that the varying state regulations do not impede interstate commerce and thus hurt the overall economy. Automobile traffic does not require this type of regulation.

48. **The correct answer is (E).** Although it may appear illogical to pay farmers not to grow crops, problems can arise from U.S. farmlands being too productive: surpluses and gluts in the market can be created, as well as situations where the excess crops have to be destroyed.

49. **The correct answer is (D).** As in the case of funds for the Contras for Nicaragua, the power of the purse is the most explicit constitutional power that Congress can exercise when it comes to foreign policy. Choice (A) is incorrect because only the Senate ratifies treaties, not the House.

50. **The correct answer is (C).** The 1980s saw the deficit balloon to an unprecedented high. This was due to deficit spending: spending money that was not available.

51. **The correct answer is (B).** The purpose of the establishment clause was to forbid the government from making any law about "an establishment of religion." Justice Black was quoting Jefferson when he said the purpose of it was to create a "wall of separation between church and state."

52. **The correct answer is (B).** *Reynolds v. United States* (1879) upheld the conviction of Reynolds, a Mormon living in Utah, for marrying two women. This happened in spite of the fact that, at the time, the Mormon church approved of polygamy.

53. **The correct answer is (A).** This is a very difficult area to pin down, mainly because the English language is not always clear. It is difficult for courts to draw the line between slander, libel, and what is acceptable as free speech. In cases such as General Westmoreland suing CBS and Ariel Sharon suing *Time* magazine, even though both CBS and *Time* were found to be in error, they were still not held financially accountable because no malicious intent was found. Courts have tended to lean toward defending free speech, even if some find it objectionable. With the information provided, choice (A) is the best choice because the accusations are the most damaging and are unsubstantiated, suggesting shoddy journalism and possible ill intent.

54. **The correct answer is (C).** Prior restraint refers to government censorship of a piece of writing before it is actually published.

55. **The correct answer is (E).** The Tenth Amendment reserves powers for the state and people. Due process protects people from unfair arrest and imprisonment. The Fourth Amendment protects against unreasonable search and seizure. The Fifth Amendment protects against double jeopardy and self-incrimination. The Sixth Amendment provides for

speedy trial and trial by jury, among other things. The Eighth Amendment protects against excessive fines and bail as well as cruel and unusual punishment.

56. **The correct answer is (D).** The concept of zones of privacy, although not stated explicitly in the Bill of Rights, is hinted at in the Ninth Amendment. Precedents such as the Privacy Act of 1974 have reinforced the idea of zones of privacy.

57. **The correct answer is (A).** The Dred Scott decision was the only decision out of the choices in which the government impeded thc progress of civil rights. The other choices were roughly a result of the Civil War and attempts after the Civil War to redress institutionalized discrimination against African-Americans.

58. **The correct answer is (B).** If one reads the Preamble to the Constitution, there is nothing discriminatory in it. The ideals behind the Constitution would have been quite noble if they were applied to all, regardless of race or sex. The Civil War shows that unity was not necessarily foremost in many people's minds. The Civil War amendments did not help to eliminate discrimination as much as they could have because prejudiced people found their ways around them.

59. **The correct answer is (C).** Although most discrimination legislation and Supreme Court cases use language that includes all races, not just minorities, reverse discrimination did not become a major issue until the Bakke case.

60. **The correct answer is (D).** This quote from President Lyndon B. Johnson expressed the basic impetus behind affirmative action: action to redress many years of racial discrimination.

NOTES

NOTES

NOTES

NOTES

NOTES

NOTES